WHO SAVES, **GOD OR ME?**

There have been many books penned about the doctrines of God's sovereign grace since the recovery of the Reformed faith began in the 1950's. However, few have clarified the essence of the debate – the nature of salvation – as clearly as Erroll Hulse has in this vital release. The writer has masterfully woven his thesis with: warm theology, pertinent church history, inspiring biography, challenges toward our responsibility, warnings of apostasy, at the same time, wrapping it all up with evangelistic urgency! Our brother has given us a powerful tool to help us articulate the doctrines of grace with the grace of the doctrines. Every evangelical Christian concerned about this generation must read this book!

JERRY MARCELLINO
Pastor of Audubon Drive Bible Church in Laurel, Mississippi, and Moderator of The Fellowship of Independent Reformed Evangelicals (FIRE)

In one word I commend most heartily this book: Excellent! Charles Spurgeon once said: 'And I have my own private opinion that there is no such a thing as preaching Christ and him crucified, unless you preach what now-a-days is called Calvinism. I have my own ideas, and those I always state boldly. It is a nickname to call it Calvinism; Calvinism is the gospel, and nothing else.' Erroll Hulse's book convincing proves the point. To understand its contents is liberating! To live by them is exhilarating! Whether we agree with Erroll Hulse or not, the truth so ably spelt out in this book will certainly prevail.

MARTIN HOLDT
Pastor of Constantia Park Baptist Church in Pretoria, South Africa

Who saves, God or me? has really warmed my heart! In this book, Erroll Hulse puts facts together that I wish Western missionaries who brought Christianity to Africa had emphasized to us from the beginning. He argues doctrinally, biblically, and historically that salvation is a work of God. We would have had much healthier churches on African soil by now if we appreciated this. True evangelicalism and, consequently, true worship hang on the question of our understanding of salvation. Realizing that our salvation is a free gift of God produces the kind of robust faith that we desperately need today. May this book find its way into every African nation and, if possible, into every African pastor's hands!

CONRAD MBEWE
Pastor of Kabwata Baptist Church in Lusaka, Zambia

Typical of Erroll Hulse, *Who saves, God or me?* is an informative and practical book that affirms the basics of the Reformed faith is a biblically balanced way. The chapters on Arminianism and Hyper-Calvinism are particularly timely. Historically, the churches that have maintained Reformed confessional theology — often summarized soteriologically in the litmus test of the 'five points' — have usually remained healthy, whereas those that have fallen into the errors of Arminianism or Hyper-Calvinism, have usually ended in liberalism or fatalism. Every Christian concerned about the church's future and about maintaining a biblical balance of truth, which gives all glory to God for salvation without negating man's full responsibility, should read this book and give a copy to as many friends as possible.

JOEL R. BEEKE
President and Professor of Systematic Theology and Homiletics at Puritan Reformed Theological Seminary in Grand Rapids, Michigan

WHO SAVES,
GOD OR ME?

Calvinism for the twenty-first century

ERROLL HULSE

PUBLISHING WITH A MISSION

PUBLISHING WITH A MISSION

EP Books
Faverdale North, Darlington DL3 0PH England
EP Books USA
P.O. Box 825, Webster NY 14580 USA
email: sales@evangelicalpress.org
www.epbooks.org

Unless otherwise indicated, all Scripture quotations are from Holy Bible, New International Version. Copyright © 1973, 1978, 1984, International Bible Society. Used by permission of Hodder & Stoughton, a member of the Hodder Headline Group. All rights reserved.

British Library Cataloguing in Publication Data available
ISBN 978 085234 685 3

PRINTED IN THE UK

CONTENTS

INTRODUCTION

Every Christian without exception needs to know where he or she stands with regard to salvation. Did I save myself or did God save me? On the day of Pentecost Peter warned his hearers and pleaded with them saying, 'Save yourselves from this corrupt generation' (Acts 2:40). It is imperative to take action and exercise faith and repentance. I save myself by obeying the gospel. I repent, and I believe. However as I look back and view my repentance and faith I ask the question, 'Was that me or was it God's gift to me?' In other words, who initiated the process, and who directed me in the first place? If it was my initiative, then I have something to boast about. However that cannot be the case, because the text of Scripture says, 'For it is by grace you have been saved, through faith — and this not from yourselves, it is the gift of God — not by works, so that no one can boast. For we are God's workmanship, created in Christ Jesus to do good works, which God prepared in advance for us to do' (Ephesians 2:8-10). Repentance is described as a gift from God (Acts 11:18). Faith too is a gift (2 Peter 1:1).

The idea has become widespread that God is sovereign in everything and he reigns in everything — with one exception, and that is the 'free will' of man. I have heard preachers place free will above the transcendence of God: 'There is one thing God cannot change, and that is your free will.' Can that be right? The transcendence of God means that he is above his creation. His immanence means that he permanently pervades the universe and that he remains in control of all the things he has created. The transcendence and immanence of God are brought together in Romans 11:36: 'For from him and through him and to him are all things. To him be the glory for ever! Amen.' Paul makes it clear that 'it is not of him who wills, nor of him who runs, but of God who shows mercy' (Romans 9:16, NKJV). Isaiah states it this way, 'Yet, O LORD, you are our Father. We are the clay, you are the potter' (Isaiah 64:8).

The idea of the supremacy of the human will in conversion carries over into churches so that the idea prevails that God is only allowed to do what *we* allow him to do. We see this in some worship songs. The supremacy of 'my will' is expressed in the chorus 'Jesus, You are changing me', but the change is under the auspices of my will. The last line reads, '*As I let you reign supreme within my heart.*' This is really idolatry and is misguided, because it is in fact exalting 'me'. Public worship is gradually moving away from being God-centred to being man-centred, with the focus on all *my* needs.

Over the past few decades, the idea of the supremacy of the human will over all things has been expressed in a new way in what is known as 'open theism'. Well-known advocates of this are John Sanders and Clark Pinnock. They argue that God does not exercise control over the universe in any absolute sense but that the future is open and free for human decisions to take place. According to this theory, *not even God knows* which way things will go in the future. Open theism is unbiblical, because it effectively deprives God of his transcendence and supremacy. Open theism would have been rejected and disowned by Arminians in the past.

GOD'S WORK OR OURS? THE FIVE POINTS

The five points of Calvinism, sometimes referred to as 'the doctrines of grace', are matters that affect the ministry and life of every local church. As such, they need to considered by each church, as every church needs a constitution that outlines its theological foundation. It is unwise to apply to a local church without knowing the doctrinal foundation of that church.

To take the matter further, every candidate for the ministry has to make up his mind where he stands concerning the doctrines of grace. He will need to investigate the doctrinal foundation of the Bible college or seminary where he studies. Some seminaries are strongly committed to the doctrines of grace. Others are eclectic, which is a way of saying that all views are taught and the student is left to choose. When my wife and I studied at the London Bible College from 1954 to 1960, the principal, Dr E. F. Kevan, was committed to the doctrines of grace and taught them clearly in the classroom.

The subject of salvation by free and sovereign grace or by free will has always been controversial in the church of Christ and likely always will be. As such, it is always relevant to pursue a clearer understanding of this issue. In addition, these doctrines help us to understand the history of Christ's church. For example, the history of Baptists in England can be seen to run in three streams: Arminian, Calvinist, and Hyper-Calvinist. Entire denominations uphold the doctrines of grace. The

Westminster Confession of Faith, which is the confession used by various Presbyterian denominations, affirms the doctrines of grace, as does the almost identical *Second London Baptist Confession of Faith of 1689*. Do these things matter? They certainly do, because they lie at the very heart of how we understand God.

So great is the impact of coming to embrace these truths that some of have suggested it is a second blessing after conversion. Certainly, in my life, I have found that to be so. Chapter 6, 'The experience of free grace', illustrates what I mean. I came to embrace the doctrines of grace through an intense study of these truths, as found in Romans 1 to 3.

In addition, many sensitive issues in the Christian life are allied to these doctrines and these are addressed in the closing chapters. Especially crucial is the issue of perseverance. Will I persevere to the end? This is made problematic by some difficult passages in Hebrews and these are addressed in chapter 11. Also, what about God's willingness to save sinners? A friend of mine in South Africa was struggling with this very issue and when I emailed him chapter 12 ('God wants you to be saved'), he found it very reassuring. My prayer is that the reader will find much encouragement and blessing in the expositions of these great doctrines.

WHAT IS SALVATION?

I f the well-known atheist Richard Dawkins is correct, then we are objects that arrived in this world by chance, and when we die we are buried and turn to dust without any salvation from death. Dawkins is a man who has no hope. By his own very dogmatic religion of atheism, there is nothing beyond the grave — just eternal dust. In other words, there is no salvation. The truth, however, is far different.

What is salvation? The word is commonly used in reference to being delivered or rescued from all kinds of adverse situations; for instance, those stranded at sea being saved by a helicopter rescue crew; or, firefighters saving people trapped inside a burning building.

In the New Testament the term 'Saviour' is ascribed to both

God and Jesus (1 Timothy 1:1; 2 Timothy 1:10). The name 'Jesus' was given to God's Son 'because he will save his people from their sins' (Matthew 1:21). The context in which 'save' is used in the New Testament refers to deliverance from sin and from the wrath of God as the ultimate fate which awaits the sinner (Romans 5:9-10). Salvation is from eternal damnation and from the fires that can never be quenched (Mark 9:48).

Christians are those people who are *certain* that they will be saved. It has sometimes been held that this concept of a future salvation is primary in the New Testament (Acts 2:21; Romans 13:11; 1 Corinthians 5:5; Hebrews 9:28; 1 Peter 1:5). However Christians are also described as 'those who are *being* saved' (Acts 2:47; 1 Corinthians 1:18; 2 Corinthians 2:15) and indeed as 'those who have *been* saved' (Ephesians 2:5,8) Thus, the moment of conversion is regarded as the moment of salvation (Acts 2:21).[1]

The use of the term salvation in itself indicates that salvation is an action that comes outside oneself — from God. 'He saved us, not because of righteous things we had done, but because of his mercy. He saved us through the washing of rebirth and renewal by the Holy Spirit' (Titus 3:5).

In order to attain eternal salvation three things are essential: justification, sanctification, and the resurrection from the dead. With regard to these essential elements of salvation it is customary to proceed first to justification, then sanctification (holiness of life), and then to the resurrection. That is the logical order, but here I will start with the resurrection and then go back to justification and sanctification.

SALVATION IS RESURRECTION FROM THE DEAD

I was born into a family that was nominally Church of England. Because of my background I am familiar with the *Book of*

---

1 I. H. Marshall, 'Salvation' in eds., Sinclair B. Ferguson and David F. Wright *New Dictionary of Theology* (Downers Grove: IVP, 1988), 610.

Common Prayer. This book is full of biblical materials, and there is a paragraph on the reality of the resurrection, which is excellent when rightly used. Sadly, it is constantly misapplied at funerals. Over the years I have attended funerals, and in every instance the following words have been used irrespective of the person being buried or cremated:

> FORASMUCH as it has pleased Almighty God of his great mercy to take unto himself the soul of our dear brother (sister) here departed, we therefore commit his (her) body to the ground; earth to earth, ashes to ashes, dust to dust; in sure and certain hope of the Resurrection to eternal life, through our Lord Jesus Christ; he will change our vile body, that it may be like unto his glorious body, according to the mighty working, whereby he is able to subdue all things to himself.[2]

This proclamation is constantly used for individuals who have evidenced no personal faith in Christ. Some have been known for the habit of habitual blasphemy of Christ's name. Many who are honoured with this grand promise of eternal life, during their lives never attended services except for a christening, a marriage service, or a funeral. It is well known that unrepentant adulterers, law-breakers, criminals, bank robbers, and paedophiles, have been honoured with the same burial promise that is recorded above.

The Bible does indeed teach a universal resurrection from the dead but it is most certainly not a universal resurrection of all the dead to eternal *life*. Jesus said, 'Do not be amazed at this, for a time is coming when all who are in their graves will hear his voice and come out — those who have done

---

2 'The Order for the Burial of the Dead' in the *Book of Common Prayer* (1662).

good will rise to live, and those who have done evil will rise to be condemned' (John 5:28-29).

To be saved is to be raised to life with a glorious resurrection body. It is salvation from the grave, and it is salvation on the great Judgement Day — salvation from God's eternal wrath.

SALVATION IS JUSTIFICATION BY FAITH

The chief place in the Bible where justification is explained is in the Epistle to the Romans. In that letter the apostle Paul shows us that men and women are lost in sin. That is not hard to believe, because the world is full of violence, crime, and war. The root problem is that we are all born with natures that are selfish and at enmity towards God. We break God's law, which is expressed in the Ten Commandments. If we die in a state of hostility towards God we will be sent to hell — a place of eternal punishment and pain. That is exceedingly bad news — but the good news is that we can be saved!

Paul introduces the subject of salvation as follows:

> I am not ashamed of the gospel, because it is the power of God for the salvation of everyone who believes: first for the Jew, then for the Gentile. For in the gospel a righteousness from God is revealed, a righteousness that is by faith from first to last, just as it is written: The righteous will live by faith (Romans 1:16-17).

Note the main reason why Paul is not ashamed. He declares, 'For in the gospel a righteousness from God is revealed.' It is that righteousness which forms the basis of God's justification. This righteousness is crucial because it has been procured at the enormous cost of Christ's painful, atoning, propitiatory death on the cross (Romans 3:21-27; 2 Corinthians 5:21). Without this righteousness procured by Christ there is no way of salvation. This is why the apostle Paul warns so strongly against tampering with the truth of justification by faith alone and by grace alone (Galatians 1:6-10).

To 'justify' in the Bible means to 'declare righteous'. That is, to declare of a man on trial that he is not liable to any penalty but is entitled to all the privileges due to those who have kept the law. Justifying is the act of a judge pronouncing the opposite sentence to condemnation — that of acquittal and legal immunity.[3]

God justifies those whom he calls, not by infusing righteousness into them, but by pardoning their sins and by accounting and accepting their persons as righteous. As we see in Romans 4:3 this has *always* been God's way of salvation: 'Abraham believed God, and it was credited to him as righteousness.'

It is not an over-simplification to say that throughout history men and women have sought to justify themselves by their own merit even though God affirms that 'no one will be declared righteous in his sight by observing the law' (Romans 3:20). Throughout their history the majority of Jews have always held to a system of merit, seeking to justify themselves before God by law-keeping (Romans 9:30–10:4). Similarly, Muslims universally follow the idea that we must strive in such a way that our merits or good works outweigh our sins and demerits. They follow the notion that God will accept those who succeed on the basis of merit.

Since justification by imputed righteousness is essential for salvation it calls for definition.

Martin Luther (1483-1546) called God's gift of righteousness 'an alien righteousness'. That is, it comes from the *outside*. It comes from God and is put around the believer. If I receive a garment made in China and I put it round me, it will be alien, because it comes from the outside. It is from another

3 J. I. Packer, *God's Words: Studies of Key Bible Themes* (Downers Grove: IVP, 1981), 139.

world. It is not of my making. We should note well that the idea of being clothed with this righteousness is expressed in Zechariah 3 and also in Revelation 3:4-5 and 7:9. 'Then each of them was given a white robe' (Revelation 6:11). So cogent was this idea in the early church that when baptismal candidates came out of the waters of baptism they would be covered with white robes.

Here are some facts about this alien righteousness which makes us acceptable before God and gives us a right to be in his family as sons and daughters:

1. This righteousness comes from God the Father. It is a *gift*.

2. This righteousness is put on us by an *act* of God the Father. It is an act not a process. It is a *once and for all act* never to be repeated. We do nothing. We believe and come into union with Christ by faith. The righteousness is then put upon us.

3. This righteousness consists of the complete and perfect life of Christ. It is the sum total of *his* obedience. He has done what we should have done. Jeremiah 23:6 summarizes the matter: 'This is the name by which he will be called: the LORD Our Righteousness.'

4. This righteousness is given because of the atonement. God's Son is the propitiation; Romans 3:21-27 explains this — the well-known Bible commentator Leon Morris suggests that this is the most important paragraph ever written. This propitiation effectively *removes the wrath of God* from the sinner.

5. There is no merit in receiving this righteousness. We receive it not because we are obedient. We receive it through faith as an instrument and not through faith as a merit.

6. This righteousness is a human righteousness. We are

human. Our sins emanate from our fallen sinful humanity. We are born with Adam's first sin imputed to us. Moreover, we are born with Adam's sinful nature. The righteousness that is the basis of our justification is the human obedience and human perfection of Christ.

SALVATION IS HOLINESS OF LIFE

If we are to be raised to eternal life from the grave we must be justified in God's sight. However, there is a further essential, because the Scripture says, 'without holiness no one will see the Lord' (Hebrews 12:14). It is hypocritical for a person to say, 'I am justified', but then live like a devil.

Essential for salvation is a holy life. How can we overcome sin and live in a way that is pleasing to God? Our union with Christ achieves both our justification and our sanctification (Romans 6:1-14). This involves the gift of the Holy Spirit. When Peter preached on the day of Pentecost he promised the gift of the person and work of the Holy Spirit to those who repented, believed, and were baptized as believers. This is what he said: 'Repent and be baptized, every one of you, in the name of Jesus Christ for the forgiveness of your sins. And you will receive the gift of the Holy Spirit' (Acts 2:38).

The gift of the Holy Spirit is subsequent upon our union with Christ. Here is the empowerment to live a life of holiness (Romans 8:1-17). A holy life includes living by the teaching of the Bible and maintaining a life of prayer: 'Man does not live on bread alone, but on every word that comes from the mouth of God' (Matthew 4:4).

SALVATION – GOD'S WORK OR OURS?

Salvation is described as having three parts: the resurrection from the dead, justification by faith, and holiness of life.

To be sure, when we are in our graves we certainly will have no part in God's work of raising us from the dead. But whose work is justification by imputed righteousness? And is holiness of life our work or God's? That is the subject of the ensuing pages.

2

ARMINIUS AND
THE SYNOD OF DORT

The sixteenth-century Dutch professor Jacobus Arminius (1560-1609) probably never dreamed that his name would be associated in one way or another with most Christians to the end of this age. Of course, not all Christians know the name 'Arminius' but all, without exception, either will hold to a view that accords with Arminianism or will firmly reject that system. The issue of Arminianism will sooner or later challenge most believers, so it is important that we understand what it was that he taught.

Arminius' teaching resulted in the convening of an international conference that took place in Dordrecht, Holland. Convened by the Dutch Reformed Church, but with representatives from eight foreign nations, this conference was unique because it concentrated on specific central truths about salvation and published those findings after it was concluded (November 1618 to May 1619).

Here we will follow the life of Arminius and see how that led to the famous Synod of Dort. The political situation in the Netherlands was complex, and patience is needed to follow that side of the story. I will conclude with an assessment of the character and doctrine of Arminius.

Jacobus Arminius, from whom Arminianism as a system of thought receives its name, was born in Oudewater, South Holland. When he was only an infant his father died, and Jacobus was then cared for by a godly, converted priest. This man died when Jacobus was only fourteen. Jacobus moved to Marburg, Germany, where news reached him in 1575 that Oudewater had been sacked, and his mother, sister and two brothers had been massacred. Jacobus then found a home with Peter Bertius, a pastor in Rotterdam. A deep friendship developed with Peter Bertius Jr. The two went to the newly formed University of Leiden, where they studied for six years. Arminius was so talented that funds were provided for him to move on to Geneva, where he pursued his theological studies under Theodore Beza (1519-1605).

In 1588 Arminius returned to Amsterdam, where he was ordained. In 1590 he married the daughter of one of Amsterdam's magistrates. It was at about that time that he found himself in trouble when he expounded the man of Romans 7 as an unregenerate man. When he came to Romans 9, he denied the doctrine of predestination and reprobation. Charges on several counts were brought against Arminius, all of which he answered well, except in the case of predestination. He displayed exceptional penetration in his arguments and was concerned to avoid any scheme in which God might appear, even by implication, the author of evil.

Arminius had admired the English Puritan William Perkins (1558-1602). However when he read Perkins' work on predestination he reacted strongly against it. He rejected the supralapsarian position of Perkins and also disagreed with the general implications of the doctrine of predestination. (Supralapsarianism has to do with the order of God's decrees.)[1]

Arminius wrote a critical reply, but when Perkins died in 1602 Arminius withheld the publication of his treatise. It was published posthumously in 1612. Richard A. Muller suggests,

> We must hypothetize a fairly long development of Arminius' thought. Not only did Arminius intentionally work through a series of key biblical and theological *loci* related to the problems of grace, human will, and predestination; he also became acquainted with a series of Lutheran and Roman Catholic views in which alternative approaches to those problems were to be found.

Thus he later commented that 'the Lutheran and Anabaptist churches as well as that of Rome' view the Reformed doctrine of predestination as erroneous, and he noted in particular the teachings of Philipp Melanchthon (1497-1560) and of the Danish theologian Niels Hemmingsen (1513-1600), as offering an alternative view.[2]

In 1602 plague desolated parts of the Netherlands. Arminius served his people faithfully throughout this time without

---

1 Infralapsarianism is: 1. Decree to create man; 2. Decree to allow Fall; 3. Decree of election and reprobation; 4. Decree to send Christ to die for the elect. Supralapsarianism is: 1. Decree of election and reprobation; 2. Decree to allow Fall; 3. Decree to send Christ to die for the elect; 4. Decree to create man. The majority of Calvinists in the history of the church, perhaps eighty percent, have been infralapsarian.

2 Thomas R. Schreiner and Bruce A. Ware, eds., *The Grace of God and the Bondage of the Will* (Grand Rapids: Baker, 1995), vol. 2, 255.

fear for his own life. The ranks of the University of Leiden were depleted by the plague and Arminius was appointed to teach there, although not without dispute over his doctrinal position. Subsequent to Arminius' teaching at Leiden there was much unrest because students began to show aberrant theological tendencies. Arminius wrote extensively and his works were published after he died in 1609 at only forty-nine years old. He left a wife and nine children. His ideas continued to spread pervasively and widely in all sectors, including among the common people.

THE REMONSTRANTS

Arminius' views represented a marked departure from Reformed teaching. He was synergistic inasmuch as he sought to combine the effectual grace of God with the free will of man. Following his death, his disciples contended for his principles. These disciples were known as the Remonstrants.

The mantle of leadership for the Remonstrants was taken up by Johannes Uytenbogaert (1557-1644) who championed the cause of freedom of speech. Uytenbogaert was a court preacher, and he shared the leadership of the Remonstrants with Simon Episcopius (1583-1643) who filled Arminius' place at the University of Leiden.

In 1610 Uytenbogaert called together forty Arminian pastors, who drew up five propositions known as the 'Five Articles of Remonstrance'. These were:

1. Election conditioned on foreseen faith.
2. Universal atonement.
3. The need for regeneration.
4. The resistibility of grace.
5. The uncertainty of the perseverance of believers.

One of these, the need of regeneration (3), is correct, but the other points were misguided and erroneous, especially in the context in which they were set. Needless to say the publication of these articles caused widespread controversy.

Prince Maurice of Nassau (1567-1625), the political leader whose role was crucial in this whole affair, remained neutral until 1616 when he joined the Calvinist party. The Prince was encouraged to call for a National Synod, which in fact became unique in Protestant history because of its international character.

The issues debated at the Synod of Dort were played out within a political context and have reference to the Twelve Years' Truce signed between Spain and the United Provinces of the Netherlands in 1609. The War Party wanted to renew the War of Independence in 1621 whereas the Peace Party desired to re-negotiate the truce and extend it. The Grand Pensionary of Holland (prime minister) was the political patron of the Arminians and also the leader of the Peace Party, whereas the *stadtholder* (head of state), Prince Maurice, became the patron of the Calvinists and also the leader of the War Party. Only by maintaining theological precision and discipline would the Calvinists be able to defend and preserve their cause. They saw the Remonstrants as representing a party that stood for a leniency that would drift back to Rome and the Empire out of which they had found a refuge.[3]

The political situation was tense. Did this affect the way in which the statements of Dort were formulated? The answer is no. Certainly there was pressure for a clear outcome, but the content of the formularies was an entirely theological matter.

---

3 Dr Charles A. McIlhenny, 'Case of Professor James Arminius and the Synod of Dort', *Reformed Theological Journal*, November 2002. This is a compact 14-page well-researched overview of the background to the Synod and summary of the five points.

THE SYNOD OF DORT

The Synod of Dort was the largest international gathering ever held within the bounds of the Reformed churches. Those who gathered to confer and respond to the five points of the Remonstrants included fifty-six ministers and ruling elders from the Dutch Reformed churches, five professors of theology, and twenty-six foreign theologians from eight other nations, including representatives from Switzerland (Zurich, Berne, and Basel) and Germany. Eighteen political commissioners who were not members of the Synod supervised the proceedings. Five delegates were appointed from England by King James (1566-1625), but as he rejected the Presbyterianism of Scotland there were no representatives from Scotland. Four highly-esteemed theologians from France were appointed to attend, but when the time came, the King of France, Henry IV (r. 1589-1610), would not allow them to go. However, after the Synod of Dort the French Reformed Church enthusiastically approved the Canons of Dort and made them binding on their ministers.

From its inception, the Remonstrants were treated as an accused party. At the twenty-second session, thirteen Remonstrants appeared before the Synod. Episcopius was their leader and spokesman. He stated their case with eloquence but gave offence by being too bold and dogmatic. He also lacked finesse and diplomacy. For instance it was not necessary for him to declare the assembly to be schismatical. Thereafter the Remonstrants were excluded. Subsequent to Dort and as an outcome of it, 200 Arminian ministers were deposed from office in the Dutch Reformed Church. During the discussions, the issues were by no means clear-cut. Delegates from other countries argued persistently for the universal sufficiency of the atonement and for the sincere intention of God in the free offer of the gospel.

The Synod was inaugurated on 13 November 1618 by a

service in 'De Groote Kerk' in the city of Dordrecht and concluded with a closing service in the same church on 9 May 1619. There were 154 sessions held in a hall that was heated throughout the winter by a great fire on a hearth. As extra protection against the cold and damp (about which many complained), each delegate was supplied with a *stoofje*, a small oven filled with hot coals to be placed under the feet. Numerous candlesticks and three great chandeliers provided adequate lighting. Twenty-four pounds of tallow (a rendered form of beef or mutton fat) was consumed every evening. Two galleries for spectators could accommodate between 400 and 500 people.

It is interesting to compare the Synod of Dort with the Westminster Assembly (1643-1649), which convened in London at the request of Parliament. There were 151 delegates appointed to Westminster, nearly all English Puritans. An average of 70 men met in 1,163 sessions. Some days were given wholly to prayer and fasting. Every Monday morning, a vow was read aloud on behalf of all attending delegates — a promise to be faithful in every respect to the Word of God. The Westminster Assembly produced a full *Confession of Faith* of thirty-three brief chapters that, with all the Scripture texts written out in full, comes to 150 pages. In comparison, the Synod of Dort produced a statement, confined mostly to the subject of salvation, which runs to about twenty-six pages. Without the Scriptures appended, the two documents come to about the same length. The Westminster divines also produced the *Larger* and *Shorter Catechisms* and the *Directory for Public Worship*.

Throughout the Synod of Dort, the crucial issue of sovereign grace was powerfully affirmed as necessary biblical truth. At the same time Arminianism was firmly rejected. The Protestant churches were strengthened as is illustrated by the fact that the Protestant Church in France required all her ministers to subscribe to the formularies of Dort. However, a very strong resurgence of Arminianism was on the way in England under the leadership of Archbishop William Laud (1573-1645).

EVALUATION OF THE LIFE AND DOCTRINE OF ARMINIUS

Jacobus Arminius was always zealous in the service of God. He was exemplary in his personal devotions and generous in his hospitality. Even his enemies could not find fault with his life and character. In spite of the controversies that raged in his life he was a man who preferred peace. As his friendship with Uytenbogaert illustrates, Arminius was faithful and devoted in personal friendships. There is no evidence that he was a man motivated by ambition for himself. He was tolerant and patient in his attitude to those who differed from him.

By far the most difficult issue to determine is to what extent Arminius knew that his teachings were not in line with the doctrinal standards that he had promised to keep. He must have been aware that he did not hold to some parts of the *Heidelberg Catechism* and the *Belgic Confession*. He was accused of duplicity on this account. He repeatedly promised not to teach anything from the pulpit or from the university chair that was not in keeping with those standards.

Dr Roger Nicole (b.1915) is esteemed as one of the foremost theologians of our times. In recent years he settled as a professor of theology at Reformed Theological Seminary in Orlando, Florida. Dr Nicole summarized the doctrinal aberrations of Arminius with outstanding insight and clarity:

> It must be owned that Arminius' views represent a clearly marked departure from the Reformed faith. In his published works we do find the seed for most, if not all, subsequent developments of the Remonstrant movement away from Reformed orthodoxy. Predesti-

nation according to foreknowledge, denial of irresistible grace, universal intention of the atonement, and
uncertainty about perseverance — these tenets, which
were to form the main points of the Remonstrance,
are clearly stated.

Deviant trends may be further observed in the matters of justification by faith, sanctification, the necessity of the gospel unto salvation, the essential deity of
Christ, and original sin. In view of the constant agita-
tion caused by those who had studied under him, it is
probable that he went further in his private contacts
than in his materials which have been published.

The charge of Pelagianism which was often pressed
against Arminius must certainly be qualified in terms
of his strong emphasis upon the need of divine grace
for any good in man. While he contended for free will,
he acknowledged the radical corruption of man and
held that no good choice could be made at any time
apart from the gracious assistance of God. The suspi-
cion that he had leanings toward Roman Catholicism
appears to have been quite without foundation.[4]

It is not surprising that Dr Nicole points out that: 'Deviant
trends may be further observed in the matters of justification
by faith, sanctification, the necessity of the gospel unto salvation, the essential deity of Christ, and original sin.'

We move forward now to briefly consider the formularies
of the Synod of Dort.

---

4   Roger Nicole, *The Encyclopedia of Christianity* (Wilmington: Delaware, 1964).

3

THE FORMULARIES OF THE SYNOD OF DORT

Foundational to our understanding of the Synod of Dort is the confession of the Remonstrants. The inspiration behind the Five Articles of the Remonstrance is that God must be protected from the charge of injustice. According to the understanding of the disciples of Arminius, Calvinism represents a view that advocates that God determines man's destiny without any regard whatever to man's works. Arminians have in their minds these questions: Is this not sheer arbitrariness? Does this not make men pawns? If God's decree is all that there is, then all history is like a video which has been pre-set.

The first point of the Remonstrants is that election is based on foreseen faith. This includes perseverance. Those who God foresaw would persevere to the end will be saved.

The second point is that Christ's atonement gained reconciliation for all men equally and without exception. It is up to individuals to make this good for themselves.

The third point is that even though fallen man is sinful, it is free will that makes the way for regeneration. When man by his free will submits, then the Holy Spirit is free to work. Free will is the cause of regeneration.

The fourth point is that grace is resistible. This is an extension of the former point. The sinner on his own initiative must will to be acceptable to God.

The fifth point concerns final perseverance. Only those who persevere by faith will be saved. On the face of it no one would disagree with that. However the issue is whether this perseverance is achieved by human effort or by the power of the Holy Spirit ensuring absolutely that the believer will persevere.

RESPONDING TO THE REMONSTRANTS: THE FORMULARIES OF THE SYNOD OF DORT

In response to the Five Articles of the Remonstrance, the Synod of Dort formulated its canons in four chapters and ninety-three articles. These were signed on 23 April and solemnly promulgated in De Groote Kerk, Dordrecht, on 6 May 1619. Three days later, after six months of hard work, the visiting theologians from other nations took their leave.

The formularies as well as the Scripture proofs have been translated from the Latin in which they were first published. It is important to capture the flavour of this work, and we can do that by a brief sketch of the formularies as follows.

ELECTION AND REPROBATION

The first main point of doctrine concerns divine election and reprobation. Eighteen articles follow. The first points to the fact that all mankind is condemned (Romans 3:19). This is followed by the citation of John 3:16 and also Romans 10:14-15, which declares the necessity of gospel preaching. The question of unbelief and gospel rejection is then addressed. This leads directly to the subject of divine election — a truth declared in Ephesians 1:4-6. Article 9 concerns the fact that election is not based on faith foreseen. Article 12 is experimental: 'How does a person recognize election? Answer: not by inquisitive searchings into the hidden things of God, but by noticing within themselves spiritual joy and holy delight, the unmistakable fruits of election pointed out in God's Word.' Pastoral sensitivity is expressed in Article 16 towards those who may have difficulty with regard to reprobation.

Article 17, 'The salvation of the infants of believers', reads as follows: 'Since we must make judgements about God's will from his Word, which testifies that the children of believers are holy, not by nature but by virtue of the gracious covenant in which they together with their parents are included, godly parents ought not to doubt the election and salvation of their children whom God calls out of this life in infancy.'

The first main section concludes with nine paragraphs that state and repudiate the errors of the Arminians.

PARTICULAR REDEMPTION

The second main point of doctrine addressed has to do with particular redemption. Having asserted the absolute necessity of the death of Christ as an atonement for sin, Article 3 states: 'This death of God's Son is the only and entirely complete sacrifice and satisfaction for sins; it is of infinite value and worth, more than sufficient to atone for the sins of the whole world.'

Article 5 stresses that the command to repent and believe ought to be announced and declared, without differentiation or discrimination, to all nations and people, and Article 8 states: 'It was God's good will through the blood of the cross to effectively redeem from every people, tribe, nation and language all those to whom he should grant faith.'

Seven paragraphs refuting the errors of the Arminians follow.

CORRUPTION, CONVERSION, AND SALVATION

The third and fourth main points of doctrine address the subject of human corruption, conversion to God and the way it occurs. Seventeen articles of explanation follow. Article 8 is particularly important since it corrects a Hyper-Calvinist distortion (see chapter 9). Article 8 reads: 'Nevertheless, all who are called through the Gospel are called seriously. For seriously and most genuinely God makes known in his Word what is pleasing to him: that those who are called should come to him. Seriously he also promises rest for their souls and eternal life to all who come to him and believe.' Hyper-Calvinists reject what they term 'well meant offers of the gospel'. They succumb to human rationalism and question how God can seriously offer the gospel to all men when he knows that he will confine its effect to the elect only.

Sections four and five conclude with nine paragraphs repudiating Arminian errors. For instance the paragraph 8 is the rejection of the notion 'that man completely thwarts his own rebirth; and, indeed, that it remains in his own power whether or not to be reborn'.

PERSEVERANCE

The fifth main point of doctrine concerns the perseverance of the saints. Fifteen articles follow. Article 4 concerns the danger of true believers falling into serious sins. Constant watchfulness is exhorted and the examples of David and Peter are recalled. Article 5 addresses the effects of serious sins: 'By such monstrous sins, however, they greatly offend God, deserve the sentence of death, grieve the Holy Spirit, suspend the exercise of faith, severely wound the conscience, and sometimes lose awareness of grace for a time — until, after they have returned to the way by genuine repentance, God's fatherly face again shines upon them.'

Article 11 points to 1 Corinthians 10:13: 'The Father of all comfort does not let them be tempted beyond what they can bear, but with the temptation also provides a way out.'

4

THE FIVE POINTS

When we stand back and view the controversy between the Arminians and Calvinists at Dort we can use a helpful acrostic — TULIP — to summarize the main issues under debate. The historical source as to who first used this acronym or acrostic[1] is unknown (and we note that TULIP will not work if we translate it into other languages).

'T', standing for *total depravity*, comes first in TULIP. This point is foundational to all that follows. Is man so plunged into sin that he cannot help himself? Is his will in bondage to

---

1 According to the *Oxford English Dictionary*, 1991, today's word is *acronym*. The first example is from 1943. The word *acrostic* goes back to 1587.

sin? Does it require a new birth from heaven if he is to be saved? It must be affirmed that total depravity does not mean that man is as bad as he possibly can be. It is evident from Scripture that men and women are able to achieve a vast amount of good (Romans 2:14) — we call that the *common grace* of God. Total depravity means that man is fallen in *all his faculties*: affections, mind, will, and conscience.

The placing of total depravity as the first point in this acrostic is helpful because once the realities of total depravity are appreciated the four points that follow fall into place. To accept the implications of the first point leads almost certainly to accept the next four without difficulty. Since fallen man is at enmity with God, hopelessly lost and unable to help himself, it follows that God must take the initiative. Jonah could not escape from the great fish that swallowed him. When he was rescued he proclaimed, 'Salvation comes from the LORD' (Jonah 2:9).

The second letter, 'U' stands for *unconditional election*. Is election based on faith foreseen or is election according to the mind and will of God without any conditions?

The third letter, 'L' stands for *limited atonement*. It is self-evident that Christ's death does not secure the salvation of all mankind. In his death Christ bore the punishment of specific sins done by specific people, to redeem those upon whom he had set his love.

The fourth letter 'I' stands for *irresistible grace* and the fifth, 'P', stands for the *perseverance of the saints*.

I will now consider the biblical data supporting each of these points, with reference to how these issues are also expressed in the *Second London Baptist Confession of Faith of 1689*. In the case of the total depravity I will describe the contest between Erasmus and Luther, because that historical event illustrates the subject vividly and helpfully.

TOTAL DEPRAVITY

In support of this assertion, the formularies of Dort cite Romans 3:10:

> As it is written: 'There is no one righteous, not even one; there is no one who understands, no one who seeks God. All have turned away, they have together become worthless; there is no one who does good, not even one.'

If there is none that seeks God, does this not raise the issue of free will? If people enjoyed free will, surely they would seek God? But they do not! In fact the mind of fallen man is hostile to God, as the Scripture declares, 'The sinful mind is hostile to God. It does not submit to God's law, nor can it do so. Those controlled by the sinful nature cannot please God' (Romans 8:7-8).

In the *1689 Confession,* chapter 9 is devoted to free will. Paragraph 3 reads:

> As the consequence of his fall into a state of sin, man has lost all ability to will the performance of any of those works, spiritually good, that accompany salvation. As a natural (unspiritual) man he is dead in sin and altogether opposed to that which is good. Hence he is not able, by any strength of his own, to turn himself to God, or even to prepare himself to turn to God (John 6:44; Romans 5:6; 8:7; Ephesians 2:1,5; Titus 3:3-5).[2]

The question of free will lies at the heart of the issue of total depravity. Either man is saved by the contribution made by his free will or he is saved by grace alone. Semi-Pelagians

---

2 *A Faith to Confess: The Baptist Confession of 1689* (Sussex: Carey Publications, 1975), 31.

and Arminians concede that grace must enable the will of man to believe. They agree that grace is involved but do not agree that the issue of salvation is decided by the will of God alone and by grace alone. For them it is not God's election that decides salvation but free will.

This matter came to the fore at the beginning of the great sixteenth-century Reformation. Desiderius Erasmus (1466-1536) was unrivalled as a scholar in the classical languages. His influence was extensive and he was universally esteemed for his great learning and for his courage in challenging the corruption of the church. It was through Erasmus that the greatest step in the development of Biblical textual criticism took place, namely, the publication of the Greek text of the New Testament. Erasmus supported Martin Luther in 1520 at a very critical juncture when a demand was made for Frederick III, Elector of Saxony, to hand over Luther as a captive to be taken to Rome. Erasmus advised Frederick that Luther was guilty: 'He has attacked the monks in their belly and the Pope in his crown.' This satire is typical of Erasmus' style. It helped Frederick to see that it was out of evil motives and envy that Luther's enemies were baying for his blood. And so Frederick staved off the demand to hand over Luther.

However the pace of the Reformation was becoming more intense and Erasmus was expected by everyone to take either one side or the other. Much pressure was placed upon Erasmus to write against Luther — even King Henry VIII (1491-1547) of England wanted him to do this. Eventually, in September 1524, Erasmus took up his pen and wrote against Luther's free grace teaching. It was published in a small book with the title, *Discussion, or Collation, concerning free will*. This placed Erasmus firmly on the side of the Roman Catholic traditional Semi-Pelagian teaching and ended his role as a mediator. Up to this point he had been like Gamaliel serving as a moderating influence.

In December 1525 Luther's answer to Erasmus, *The Bondage of the Will,* was published. This treatise of about 320 pages is regarded as Luther's greatest work. In it, Luther analyzes Erasmus' reasoning, establishing from Scripture that fallen man is indeed in bondage to sin and this is manifested in the bondage of his will. He also congratulates Erasmus, declaring,

> You alone have attacked the real thing that is the essential issue. You have not worried me with those extraneous issues about the Papacy, purgatory, indulgences and such like — trifles, rather than issues — in respect of which almost all to date have sought my blood — you, and you alone, have seen the hinge on which all turns, and aimed for the vital spot.

Chapter 6, paragraph 4 of the *1689 Confession* explains why fallen man has no free will towards God.

> The actual sins that men commit are the fruit of the corrupt nature transmitted to them by our first parents. By reason of this corruption, all men become wholly inclined to all evil; sin disables them. They are utterly indisposed to, and, indeed, rendered opposite to all that is good (Matthew 15:19; Romans 8:7; Colossians 1:21; James 1:14).[3]

This paragraph points to wording of the *Westminster Larger Catechism*, Question 25: 'Wherein consists the sinfulness of that estate whereinto man fell?' Answer:

> The sinfulness of that estate whereinto man fell, consists in the guilt of Adam's first sin, the want of that

3 *A Faith to Confess,* 25-26

righteousness wherein he was created, and the corruption of his nature, whereby he is utterly indisposed, disabled, and made opposite to all that is spiritually good, and wholly inclined to all evil, and that continually; which is commonly called *Original Sin*, and from which do proceed all actual transgressions (Romans 5:12,19; 3:10-19; Ephesians 2:1-3; Romans 5:6; 8:7-8; Genesis 6:5; James 1:14-15; Matthew 15:19).

The central issue is: 'and made opposite to all that is spiritually good'. The conclusion to which we are led is that total depravity means a spiritual *inability* and spiritual *enmity* towards God. Bondage of the fallen will is such that there is *total spiritual inability* in the sinner. This inability does not mean that fallen sinners are not responsible. There are many things that unconverted men can and must do. They can abandon perverse company. They can expose themselves to searching preaching. They can side with the godly. They can quit excuses. They can confess their sins. They can call on God for the will-power that they lack for repentance and that they must have for salvation. They can pray, 'Turn me and I will be turned.' The doctrine of total depravity or human inability must never be taught in such a way as to encourage excuses such as, 'Well, there is nothing *I* can do!'

Many exhortations employed by the prophets and apostles show that sinners are in no way absolved of their responsibility because of their inability. That inability is a sinful inability. God commands the sinner: 'Cast away from you all your transgressions which you have committed, and make yourselves a new heart and a new spirit!' (Ezekiel 18:31, NASB). All that is needed for salvation, including all needed resolution to quit sin, is found in the work of the Holy Spirit. Hence the exhortation, 'Turn to my reproof, Behold, I will pour out my spirit on you' (Proverbs 1:23, NASB).

At Pentecost, the apostle Peter exposed that awful sin of which many of them were guilty, namely that of endorsing the rejection, humiliation, and crucifixion of Jesus. Peter exhorted them, 'Save yourselves from this corrupt generation' (Acts 2:40).

In his sermon 'Free-will — a Slave',[4] C. H. Spurgeon (1834-1892) shows how the reality of the bondage of the will must encourage preachers to hold forth the Prince of Life as the Liberator and Saviour — those who look to him will be saved.

UNCONDITIONAL ELECTION

Sermons on election are so rare that a regular churchgoer may never hear one. Yet the doctrine appears frequently in Scripture. Any preacher setting out to preach a series of sermons on Ephesians will be faced with election by verse four of the first chapter. The deep teaching of Ephesians may be so daunting to him that the preacher might turn away from that letter and turn instead to something easier, like Paul's first letter to the Thessalonians. But here again by the fourth verse of chapter one he is confronted head-on by election: 'For we know, brothers loved by God, that he has chosen you' (1 Thessalonians 1:4). Since Paul starts his letter in that way we can note that election is not a dangerous truth that he thinks should be hidden. Further, in his second letter to the Thessalonians the apostle Paul expresses thankfulness for the truth of election: 'But we ought always to thank God for you, brothers loved by the Lord, because from the beginning God chose you to be saved through the sanctifying work of the Spirit and through belief in the truth' (2 Thessalonians 2:13).

The doctrine may be defined as follows: Election is an act of God's free grace whereby from before the creation of the world he chose individuals to be saved, not on account of any

4 Delivered on 2 December 1855 [C. H. Spurgeon, *New Park Street Pulpit* (Grand Rapids: Baker, 1990), vol. 1, 395-408].

merit or disposition foreseen in them but only because of his sovereign purpose and good pleasure.

In Ephesians Paul says that God acted for us before the beginning of time:

> Praise be to the God and Father of our Lord Jesus Christ, who has blessed us in the heavenly realms with every spiritual blessing in Christ. For he chose us in him before the creation of the world to be holy and blameless in his sight. In love he predestined us to be adopted as his sons (Ephesians 1:3-5).

This is full of comfort for the believer. The Father chose us 'in Christ'. Election is 'in Christ' which means that every conceivable provision has been made. In his wisdom the Father has made Christ to be our 'righteousness, holiness and redemption' (1 Corinthians 1:30). Not only so, but our election in Christ means that we are united to him in the closest conceivable spiritual union. We enter into the experience of the love of Christ for us which is 'as strong as death... many waters cannot quench love, rivers cannot wash it away' (Song of Solomon 8:6-7). God's love is unchanging. We reciprocate: 'We love him because he first loved us' (1 John 4:19, NKJV). It is through our union with Christ that we are enabled to love each other in the Christian family (1 John 4:19-21).

Every time the apostle Paul uses his favourite expression, 'in Christ' — and he does it about fifty times — it is a reminder of election, because the Father chose us before the foundation of the world to be 'in Christ'. It is on account of our union with Christ that we will be made like him (Romans 8:29). Election exalts the grace of God and humbles sinners. It brings them to an end of themselves and causes them to rely only on God's mercy and grace.

Paul uses election to humble the deeply divided Corinthian church. The believers there were boastful and party-minded:

> Brothers, think of what you were when you were called. Not many of you were wise by human standards; not many were influential; not many were of noble birth. But God chose the foolish things of the world to shame the wise; God chose the weak things of the world to shame the strong. He chose the lowly things of this world and the despised things — and the things that are not — to nullify the things that are, so that no one may boast before him (1 Corinthians 1:26-29).

It is the work of God the Father that we are in Christ who is our righteousness, and sanctification and redemption so, 'Let him who boasts boast in the Lord' (1 Corinthians 1:31).

Election does not result in carelessness. Peter says we must be eager to make our calling and election sure (2 Peter 1:10). That involves adding to our faith goodness, knowledge, self-control, perseverance, godliness, brotherly kindness, and love (2 Peter 1:5-9).

The Congregationist author and hymnwriter Josiah Conder (1789-1855) sums up the truth of election like this:

> My Lord, I did not choose you,
>   for that could never be;
> This heart would still refuse you
>   had you not chosen me.
> You took the sin that stained me,
>   you cleansed and made me new;
> For you of old ordained me
>   that I should live for you.

LIMITED ATONEMENT (PARTICULAR REDEMPTION)

Particular redemption, or the fact that Christ died infallibly to secure the salvation of those whom the Father had given him, is a very important doctrine, the value and usefulness of which can be determined by each context in which it appears. For instance, Ephesians 5:25, 'Husbands, love your wives, just as Christ loved the church and gave himself up for her', expresses particular redemption. Husbands are to love their wives as Christ loved the church, so much so that he died for her. In Acts 20:28 Paul exhorts the Ephesian elders: 'Be shepherds of the church of God, which he bought with his own blood.' This exhortation reminds us of the effectiveness of Christ's sacrifice to achieve redemption.

The Synod of Dort rejected the idea that God the Father appointed the Lord Jesus Christ to die on a cross without a fixed plan to save anyone. In other words the Synod rejected the idea that Christ died merely to make persons saveable. The formularies at this point go on to show from Scripture that this is false. The Saviour speaks as follows: 'I know my sheep… and I lay down my life for the sheep' (John 10:14-15). The Synod also quoted Isaiah 53:10: 'He will see his offspring and prolong his days, and the will of the LORD will prosper in his hand.' Here we are reminded that the Messiah would lay down his life for his offspring — that is for the ones he himself described as those the Father *gave* him. His death was substitutionary, and it was vicarious, which means 'in their place'.

The formularies go further at this point to remind us all that a covenant is involved, citing Hebrews 7:22, the terms of the new covenant are decisive: 'Christ is the mediator of a new covenant, that those who are called may receive the promised inheritance' (Hebrews 9:15), and that this takes effect in the death of Christ: 'A will is in force only when somebody has died' (Hebrews 9:17). In other words, Christ's death is effectual for his people. This is what we call *particular* redemption or *definite* atonement.

The Synod also cites Galatians 2:20 where the apostle Paul declares of Christ: 'who loved me and gave himself for me'.

The atonement of Christ is limited in its efficacy to those who are saved. But the word 'limited' is unfortunate as it can convey the notion of inadequacy in the atonement. J. I. Packer, in his brilliant essay introducing a 1959 Banner of Truth edition of John Owen's treatise *The Death of Death in the Death of Christ*, stresses that Calvinism is much broader than five points. He suggests that the five points can 'present Calvinistic soteriology in a negative and polemical form, whereas Calvinism in itself is essentially expository, pastoral and constructive'. He points out that the word *limited*, 'is often read with stress on the adjective and taken as indicating that Calvinists have a special interest in confining the limits of divine mercy'.

For centuries English Baptists have been known either as Particular Baptists or General Baptists. Particular stands for particular redemption and General for a general or universal atonement. Since the 1970s Particular Baptists have preferred the title Reformed Baptists which denotes the fact that they adhere to a Reformed confession of faith. With regard to the atonement, the term 'definite atonement' is to be preferred to the term 'limited atonement'. There are several passages and statements in Scripture that affirm the absolute efficacy of Christ's atonement for those chosen by the Father to be 'in him'. One such is Hebrew 10:14: 'because by one sacrifice he has made perfect forever those who are being made holy'. We are informed here of a Saviour whose sacrifice actually saves souls, not a sacrifice that merely makes salvation possible.

If we take up the idea that Christ died to make salvation possible on condition of a response; what then? Imagine a poll. Everyone is given a voting slip. The issue for everyone is either Christ or the world. Imagine every voting slip returned marked for the world and not one for Christ! What then? We have already considered the assertion of Paul, 'there is no one who understands, no one who seeks God. All have turned away, they have together become worthless' (Romans 3:11–12). On this basis nobody will vote for Christ. Heaven will be empty! But an effectual sacrifice has been made and has been accepted. Sinners are saved because all three Persons of the Trinity are working for their salvation.

John Owen (1616-1683) wrote extensively on this subject.[5] At one point he expressed the issue of definite atonement in a way that is hard to refute:

> God imposed his wrath due unto, and Christ underwent the pains of hell for, either [1] all the sins of all men, or [2] all the sins of some men, or [3] some sins of all men. If the last, some sins of all men, then have all men some sins to answer for, and so shall no man be saved; for if God enter into judgement with us, though it were with all mankind for one sin, no flesh should be justified in his sight: 'If the Lord should mark iniquities, who could stand?' Psalm 130:3… If the second… Christ in their stead and room suffered for all the sins of all the elect in the world. If the first, why then are not all freed from the punishment of their sins? You will say, 'Because of their unbelief; they will not believe.' But this unbelief, is it a sin, or not? If not, why should they be punished for it? If it be, then

---

5 John Owen deserves the title 'the Prince of the Puritans'. Today his writings are available in twenty-three volumes. Together they form the best resource for theology in the English language. The first writing that came from Owen was the title *A Display of Arminianism*. That is found in volume 10 of his published works (Banner of Truth) and it is followed by a 290-page classic work on particular redemption with the title *The Death of Death in the Death of Christ*. Owen begins by demonstrating that salvation is a work which involves the three Persons of the Trinity. It is a work to save a people who have been given to Christ.

Christ underwent the punishment due to it, or not. If so, then why must that hinder them more than their other sins for which he died from partaking of the fruit of his death? If he did not, then did he not die for all their sins.[6]

Owen is perceptive to observe that the sin of unbelief must be removed. As a believer I own that Christ died to take away all my sins, starting with the cardinal sin of unbelief.

While we are grateful for teachers whose writings have brought clarity and stability to the churches over the centuries we must strive to base our beliefs firmly in Scripture, as they did.

There are also examples in the Old Testament of definite atonement. For instance, when the children of Israel came out of Egypt it was essential that the blood of a lamb be daubed on the doorposts and lintels of their homes for their firstborn to be spared the sword of death (Exodus 12).

In the well known fourth Servant passage of Isaiah (52:13-53:12) the personal pronouns used in the third of the five stanzas point to definite personal atonement:

> Surely he took up our infirmities and carried our sorrows, yet we considered him stricken by God, smitten by him, and afflicted. But he was pierced for our transgressions, he was crushed for our iniquities; the punishment that brought us peace was upon him, and by his wounds we are healed. We all, like sheep, have gone astray, each of us has turned to his own way; and the LORD has laid on him the iniquity of us all (Isaiah 53:4-6).

---

6 John Owen, *The Death of Death in the Death of Christ* (Edinburgh: The Banner of Truth Trust, 1963), 61.

Our Lord makes it quite clear that he lays down his life for his sheep — those whom the Father has given him (John 10:11). In the same context he declares of those who do not believe in him: 'But you do not believe because you are not my sheep' (John 10:26).

Personal definite atonement is expressed in Ephesians 5:2: 'Christ loved us and gave himself up for us as a fragrant offering and sacrifice to God.' And in the same chapter we read, 'Christ loved the church and gave himself up for her' (Ephesians 5:25).

Charles Spurgeon stated the case like this:

> We are often told that we limit the atonement of Christ, because we say that Christ has not made a satisfaction for all men, or all men would be saved. Now our reply to this is that on the other hand, our opponents limit it: we do not. The Arminians say, Christ died for all men. Ask them what they mean by it. Did Christ die so as to secure the salvation of all men? They say, 'No, certainly not.' We ask them the next question. Did Christ die so as to secure the salvation of any man in particular? They answer, 'No.' They are obliged to admit this if they are consistent. They say, 'No. Christ has died that any man may be saved if — ' and then follow certain conditions of salvation. Now, who is it that limits the death of Christ? Why you. You say that Christ did not die so as to infallibly secure the salvation of anybody. We beg your pardon; when you say we limit Christ's death, we say, 'No, my dear sir, it is you that do it.' We say that Christ so died that he infallibly secured the salvation of a multitude that no man can number, who through Christ's death not only may be saved, but are saved, must be saved and cannot by any possibility run the hazard of being anything but saved. You are welcome to your atonement;

you may keep it. We will never renounce ours for the sake of it.[7]

The truth of definite atonement is important because it strengthens the believer's grasp on the doctrines of grace. There is unity in the doctrines. Clarity about definite atonement empowers the reality that Christ really saves. '[Christ] is able to save completely those who come to God through him' (Hebrews 7:25). Definite atonement strengthens the believer's assurance because he is held in the firm grasp of God's saving action. He is held firm by an atonement that is effective for him for time and eternity. This is not a speculation. This is a reality.

The doctrine of definite atonement is vital because it is biblical and because it can be used to refute the heresy of universal salvation and refute those who teach inclusivism. Definite atonement stands in opposition to the view of universal atonement. Many passages in Scripture like Matthew 25 and Revelation 20 show that it is absurd to believe that all will be saved. Inclusivism is the idea that in a mysterious way those of other religions are joined to Christ even though they do not know it. There is nothing in the Bible to support such assertions.

Definite atonement inspires missionary work to the ends of the earth because of the certainty of God's purpose to save his people in all nations. We read in Revelation 5:9-10:

> And they sang a new song: 'You are worthy to take the scroll and to open its seals, because you were slain, and with your blood you purchased men for God from every tribe and language and people and nation.

---

7 For a brief statement of Spurgeon's view of Calvinism and particular redemption see 'A Defence of Calvinism', in C. H. Spurgeon, *The Early Years* (Edinburgh: The Banner of Truth Trust, 1962).

You have made them to be a kingdom and priests to
serve our God, and they will reign on the earth.'

The sufficiency of the atonement is never a question in the
New Testament. There is never a hint that there is not enough
room for sinners or not adequate atonement made for their
sins. The very way in which passages are worded assures all
that there is room. 'He is the atoning sacrifice for our sins,
and not only for ours but also for the sins of the whole
world' (1 John 2:2). Whether we take the word 'world' to
mean all the Gentiles as well as the Jews, or simply a term to
embrace all peoples whatsoever, the meaning of all-sufficiency
is conveyed. All who repent and believe will be accepted.
'Turn to me and be saved, all you ends of the earth; for I am
God and there is no other' (Isaiah 45:22) conveys the message
that there is room for everyone. This is the text that took hold
of the young Spurgeon in his conversion. Jesus himself assures
us that 'whoever comes to me I will never drive away' (John
6:37). To summarize, the atonement is effectual only for those
who believe, yet when we address the unbelieving world we
urge them all, everyone, to come to Christ and trust in him.
We do so not only because their personal need is desperate
but because salvation is full and free and all-sufficient for all
who repent and believe.

It is never necessary, nor ever found in Scripture, for us to
assert that Christ died effectually for every person. That is
confusing because it is patently obvious to everyone that only
believers are saved. Spurgeon is correct in deriding a general
atonement, which in actual fact does not achieve salvation. A
bridge that only goes halfway over a river is useless.

IRRESISTIBLE GRACE
The gospel invitations are to be proclaimed to all the world and
addressed to everyone who hears the message. All without

exception are invited to come and drink the water of life freely. With this universal call goes an *effectual call* by which the Holy Spirit performs a work of grace within the sinner. He is drawn to Christ. His understanding is enlightened, his will is renewed, and he is convicted of his need to repent and believe. Fallen men and women resist the convicting work of the Holy Spirit. Hence Genesis 6:3: 'My Spirit will not contend with man forever.' At the time of his martyrdom Stephen said of his hostile Jewish persecutors that they always resisted the Holy Spirit (Acts 7:51). But God's saving grace overcomes this resistance.

Irresistible grace is described as a call that comes from God the Father: 'God, who has called you into fellowship with his Son, Jesus Christ our Lord, is faithful' (1 Corinthians 1:9). The effectual calling of God the Father is expressed in 2 Timothy 1:9: '[God] who has saved us and called us to a holy life — not because of anything we have done but because of his own purpose and grace. This grace was given us in Christ Jesus before the beginning of time.' This effectual call of the Father can be expressed in terms of the new birth. Hence, 'Praise be to the God and Father of our Lord Jesus Christ! In his great mercy he has given us new birth into a living hope through the resurrection of Jesus Christ from the dead' (1 Peter 1:3).

Irresistible grace is likened to the wind. According to the words of our Lord Jesus, the Holy Spirit blows where he will to bring new birth (John 3:8). In chapter 10 of the *1689 Confession of Faith*, irresistible grace is expressed by the term 'effectual calling'. In the first paragraph the issue is summed up in the words: 'God takes away their heart of stone and gives them a heart of flesh' (Ezekiel 36:26).

The term 'irresistible' can be misunderstood. The grace of new birth or regeneration is not brought about by compulsion or by force. The sinner comes to Christ freely. But, according to Scripture, that willingness to come to Christ and trust him wholly is in its totality due to the work of the Holy Spirit (Ephesians 2:1-10). Regeneration precedes repentance and faith, as is seen in John 1:12-13 — we receive Christ and become children of God having been 'born not of blood, nor of the will of the flesh, nor of the will of man, but of God' (NASB). Jesus said, 'No one can come to me unless the Father who sent me draws him' (John 6:44). In that drawing there is a spiritual resurrection, a new birth, a change of nature by which the sinner becomes willing to commit himself to Christ.

In regeneration there is an enlightenment of the mind so that a person can now see the kingdom and understand spiritual things. The natural man without this enlightenment 'does not accept the things that come from the Spirit of God, for they are foolishness to him, and he cannot understand them, because they are spiritually discerned' (1 Corinthians 2:14). Both the mind and the heart are regenerated by the Holy Spirit. An unregenerate sinner will not be happy to live in God's courts. But when he is born again he will say, 'How lovely is your dwelling place, O Lord Almighty' (Psalms 84:1) for 'blessed are those you choose and bring near to live in your courts' (Psalm 65:4).

The matter can be stated like this: Jesus said, 'You are unwilling to come to me so that you may have life' (John 5:40, NASB):

1. All are unwilling to come.
2. God is willing to receive all who will come.
3. Men must be made willing to come.

The words of Stephen Charnock (1628-1680) help to enlighten this point:

> The Holy Spirit removes the prejudices against Christ as undesirable, against holiness as troublesome; takes down the strength of corrupt reasonings, pulls down

those idols of the mind, and false notions of happiness, out-reasons men out of their inward thoughts of a happiness in sensual pleasures, pride of life, mammon of honour and wealth, which are the root of our spiritual disease, and first to be cured.[8]

There is a preparatory work to the new birth, which John Owen reduces to three aspects: illumination, conviction, and reformation.[9] But the actual new birth is a spontaneous supernatural work, described as a new creation (2 Corinthians 5:17; Ephesians 2:1). The sovereignty of God in this new creation is clearly asserted in Scripture: 'God made you alive with Christ' (Colossians 2:13) and, 'For we are God's workmanship, created in Christ Jesus to do good works' (Ephesians 2:10).

This omnipotent work of new birth is hidden and mysterious. As Jesus says, the Holy Spirit is like the wind, which you cannot see although you see its effects — as on the day of Pentecost when 3,000 were wonderfully converted! God does use means in the new birth: 'He chose to give us birth through the word of truth' (James 1:18) and 'for you have been born again, not of perishable seed, but of imperishable, through the living and enduring word of God' (1 Peter 1:23). The prayers of believers are included in God's purpose to call out from all nations a people for himself. The advance of the gospel throughout the world is part of God's grand purpose to bring glory to Christ and reward him for his suffering (Psalm 22:27; Isaiah 53:11-12; 54; 55).

The new birth is a change of nature described as the removal of the heart of stone (Ezekiel 36:26) and as the circumcision

---

8 For Stephen Charnock on regeneration, see Edward Parsons, ed., *Works of Stephen Charnock* (1815 edition), vol. 5, 67. Charnock's *Works* have been republished by the Banner of Truth.

9 *The Works of John Owen* (Edinburgh: The Banner of Truth Trust, 1965), vol. 3, 231.

of the heart (Deuteronomy 30:6). The new birth is also described as a cleansing from sin (Titus 3:5; John 3:5). It is a renewal of the mind and of the heart.

Such is the extraordinary nature of the new birth that the heart is changed completely from alienation to reconciliation through Christ. Initially this is seen in a drawing work (John 6:44). To quote Charnock again: 'An inexpressible sweetness allures the soul, and an unconquerable power draws the soul; there are clear demonstrations, charming persuasions, and invincible efficacy combined together in this work.'[10] It is the work of creation by the Spirit (Ephesians 2:10). It is the implanting of a new spiritual nature which the Scriptures call a new heart and which is the essence of the new covenant: 'This is the covenant I will make with the house of Israel after that time, declares the Lord. I will put my laws in their minds, and write them upon their hearts. I will be their God, and they will be my people' (Hebrews 8:10). This change is permanent. Once a person is born again, he or she cannot be 'unborn' again. 'I will inspire them to fear me, so that they will never turn away from me' (Jeremiah 32:40).

The precise time of this momentous change is known by some but cannot be pinpointed by others. In all who are born again there is a faith union with Christ. They believe that he is the God-man (1 John 5:1). They have an ability to have done with sin (1 John 3:9), to overcome the world (1 John 5:4), and they love the family of God (1 John 4:7).

The work of regeneration can be illustrated by nations at war. We often recall D-Day in 1944 when the massed allied forces were ready to invade France and were faced by a vast network of determined resistance: barbed wire, massive fortresses with gun emplacements, mine fields, artillery, tank, and infantry regiments — in short, the fierce war machine of

10 Charnock, *Works*, vol. 5, 81.

Hitler's Third Reich. Suppose on that momentous occasion that a secret peace delegation arrived behind these lines and convinced the Nazi generals that Hitler was like Satan, their cause wicked, their situation not only wicked but doomed and that they should repent and fully surrender forthwith and save their own lives and the lives of their soldiers. Suppose that from the heart those generals were convinced inwardly and persuaded and agreed to the terms offered. Would that not have been an astounding event?

But every conversion is like that because every sinner has his barbed wire defences, his guns and his artillery, and every sinner has surrounded his soul with defensive and aggressive anti-God arguments and his own war machine of resistance. No sinner is neutral. That sinners are neutral is a myth. The Holy Spirit alone can breach the aggressive defences of the sinner's soul and work a work of new birth, bringing the war with God to an end. The illustration used with regard to D-Day, like all illustrations, is limited. It would take more than the skills of a peace delegation to convince Nazi generals. A powerful inward work that could only come from God would be necessary. Nothing else would avail. Although the new birth, repentance, and faith come together, the work of the Holy Spirit in the new birth must be first, or prior, for it is by him that saving faith and repentance are wrought. It is God who takes the initiative. Jeremiah 31:19 points well to the source of repentance and accurately depicts the struggle that goes on in repentance: 'After I strayed, I repented; after I came to understand, I beat my breast. I was ashamed and humiliated because I bore the disgrace of my youth' (Jeremiah 31:19).

PERSEVERANCE OF THE SAINTS

At the outset it is essential that eternal security be carefully distinguished from the perseverance of the saints. It is clear from such promises as John 10:28-29, that our Lord wants us to know that we are eternally secure in him. He says, 'and I give eternal life to them, and they will never perish; and no one shall snatch them out of my hand. My Father, who has given them to me is greater than all; and no one is able to snatch them out of the Father's hand' (NASB). If we view our salvation from God's viewpoint it is transparent that he will achieve his purpose to save us. For instance, we have the declaration of Paul in his letter to the Philippians, 'He who began a good work in you will perfect it until the day of Christ Jesus' (Philippians 1:6, NASB).

The elect certainly are secure in Christ and once united to him as expressed in their baptism into his death, burial, and resurrection, can never be disunited from him again. However the elect must endure hardship and tribulation (John 16:33). Patience and endurance are essential.

There are places in the Bible where the emphasis is very firmly on what believers must *do*. They are in a spiritual war. At times the battle is severe and stretches them to the limit. Jesus warned of this: 'All men will hate you because of me, but he who stands firm to the end will be saved' (Matthew 10:22).

Of the five points of Calvinism, perseverance is the one that especially relates to Christian practice. Perseverance is the work of all God's children. We must persevere.

A principal concern of the formularies of Dort on perseverance is the reality of remaining sin in believers and the danger of backsliding and falling into serious sins and the effects of such serious sins (5th main point, Articles 4 and 5). There are many passages in Scripture that emphasize that saints will be sustained in their trials so that they will not fall away (Isaiah 43:1-3; 54:10; Jeremiah 32:40; Matthew 18:12-14; John 17:11,12,15). There is also that assurance: 'No temptation has seized you except what is common to man. And God is faithful; he will not let you be tempted beyond what can bear. But when you are tempted, he will provide a way out so that you can stand up under it' (1 Corinthians 10:13). This promise affirms again that God's people will persevere through trials. They are given the abilities to do so by the power of the Holy Spirit.

Chapter 17 of the *1689 Confession of Faith* lays out the truth of the perseverance of the saints in three paragraphs. The first affirms that God's elect are those to whom saving faith has been given so that they cannot totally or finally fall away. They will persevere because he continues to beget in them faith, repentance, love, joy, hope, and all the graces of the Spirit that issue from eternal life. This is precisely in line with the primary concern of Dort with regard to perseverance.

The second paragraph points to the theological undergirding of perseverance. It is not on account of free will that saints persevere but because of the immutability of God's decree of salvation, the unchangeable love of the Father, our union with the Son, and the perpetual indwelling of the Holy Spirit (Romans 5:9-10).

The third paragraph returns to the central concern in the expression of Dort, namely that it is possible for the saints to fall into sin to their own pain and hurt and that of others, yet their faith and repentance will be renewed as many examples show. The *1689 Confession* cites the examples of David (Psalm 51) and also of Peter, who fell grievously, but our Lord prayed for him and he was restored.

The statements of Hebrews 6:4-6 and Hebrews 10:29-30 seem to contradict the doctrine of perseverance. But it is important to note that these describe those who professed to be regenerate and who seemed to have the marks of regeneration but were in fact not regenerate. In addition there is 2 Peter 2:20 which tells of those who have escaped the defilement of the world by a knowledge of Christ but are again entangled and place themselves beyond recovery. These, like those described in Hebrews, are lost irreparably.

It can be reasoned, Does this not contradict perseverance? In the latter case 2 Peter 2:20 gives us a clue. The text says that the sow returns to wallowing in the mire. No radical change has taken place. The sow is a sow still. The influences of the gospel can be powerful and seemingly effective but in some cases there is no radical change of nature.

CONCLUSION

The five points of Calvinism underline the fact that sinners cannot save themselves. Our Saviour was given the name Jesus because he will save his people from their sins (Matthew 1:21). The first point, total depravity, tells us that sinners cannot save themselves. The four points that follow tell out the certainty of salvation.

In the town of Otley, in Yorkshire, England, a group of anxious onlookers surrounded a man who was lying down flat with his hand down a rainwater drain. Among the onlookers was a mother duck expressing deep alarm. She had been leading her ducklings along the gutter and hopped over the drain, but one by one her ducklings had fallen in. One by one, the man retrieved them. All ten of them were brought up unscathed and happily followed the mother duck down to the Wharfe River. There is no way that they could have come out of that drain on their own. Power of a greater kind than duck-power was needed. In the case of our salvation we must affirm that it comes entirely from an omnipotent, gracious God.

5

THE VIEWS
OF JOHN CALVIN

E ven though John Calvin (1509-1564) died fifty-four years before the Synod of Dort, his name has been associated with the five points. They are nearly always called 'The five points of Calvinism' even though Calvin had nothing to do with the formulation of them.

On 16 October 1551 a dramatic confrontation occurred in Geneva between John Calvin and Jerome Bolsec (d.1584) over the doctrine of predestination.

Jerome Bolsec, a Carmelite monk and doctor of theology in Paris, was drawn to the Reformation and so forced to leave France. By early 1551 he had settled in the canton of Geneva working as a physician. He became critical of Calvin's doctrine of predestination. It was a Friday evening when one of the Genevan ministers at a regular meeting for a sermon and discussion preached on predestination. Bolsec, who seemed to think that Calvin himself was absent, criticized Calvin and his doctrine of predestination very sharply. In response Calvin rose and gave a brilliant defence of predestination. Calvin's teaching on this subject is clearly unpacked in his systematic theology popularly know as the *Institutes*.

As we would expect, Calvin's teaching anticipates the formularies of Dort, including the doctrine of God's love for all mankind and the free, unfettered, and uninhibited offers of the gospel to sinners.

In his commentary on Romans 5:18, Calvin writes:

> Paul makes grace common to all men, not because it in fact extends to all, but because it is offered to all. Although Christ suffered for the sins of the world, and is offered by the goodness of God without distinction to all men, yet not all receive him.

Note Calvin uses the word 'offered'. Also noteworthy is his concept of God's goodness, which is consistent with his belief in common grace. The goodness of God is given to all mankind, not the elect only.

Calvin's concept of common grace has been the subject of intense study. The most comprehensive work ever written on the subject of common grace is in Dutch by theologian Abraham Kuyper (1837-1920). Another important work discussing the various positions held on common grace is *Common Grace and the Gospel* by Cornelius Van Til (1895-1987).[1] Writers on this subject refer to Calvin's recognition that any good in mankind, including religious aspiration, decent

---

1   Cornelius Van Til, *Common Grace and the Gospel* (Phillipsburg: P&R Publishing Co., 1972).

behaviour, social brotherliness, artistic and scientific achievement, is bestowed by God. There are many such references in Calvin's *Institutes*.[2]

In Calvin's commentary on Matthew 23:37 ('O Jerusalem, Jerusalem... how often I have longed to gather your children together, as a hen gathers her chicks under her wings, but you were not willing') he suggests that we have here a lament which expresses a 'maternal kindness'. He writes as follows:

> In a manner of speaking, God bares his breast to us in the overtures of the gospel...Indeed, it is precisely the tender-heartedness of God's lament in the Person of his Son that renders human unbelief in response to the gospel such a monstrous thing. For this reason — the sinner's stubborn refusal to respond appropriately to God's kind overtures — a dreadful vengeance awaits us as often as the teaching of his gospel is put before us, unless we quietly hide ourselves under his wings, in which he is ready to take us up and shelter us.[3]

In his lectures on Ezekiel, Calvin expressly states that God announces through the prophet, 'his wish is that all should be saved' (Ezekiel 18:23,32). Likewise on 2 Peter 3:9 Calvin observes:

> Though God has secretly determined to save the elect alone, he declares in the gospel that he desires the salvation of all. The only solution open to us is to acknowledge that in his revealed will God stretches

---

2 John Calvin, *Institutes of the Christian Religion* (London: Westminster Press, 1960), vol. 1, 276.

3 With regard to the tender-heartedness of God, Don Carson speaks of God's yearning, inviting, seeking love and he refers to John 3:16 and Ezekiel 33 [D. A. Carson, *Love in Hard Places* (Milton Keynes/Carlisle: Paternoster, 2002), 15].

out his hand to all alike, even though secretly he has determined to save one and not another. Nonetheless, there is no ultimate disharmony between God's purpose of election and the universal call of the gospel, however difficult this harmony may be for us to comprehend.

Calvin does not expound the extent of the atonement. Efforts have been made to determine Calvin's view on that subject by referring to his commentaries. Dr R. T. Kendall claimed that Calvin believed in an unlimited atonement, which is the view of Paul Van Buren, J. W. Anderson, and Curt Daniel. A. A. Hodge, Robert Godfrey, and Roger Nicole maintain that Calvin did believe in a limited atonement. S. J. Hayhow in an article in the *Banner of Truth* magazine (Issue 330) maintains that Calvin implicitly held to particular atonement. His citation of Calvin shows that Calvin certainly held to the sufficiency of the atonement for all. In another article in the same magazine (Issue 398), Iain Murray refutes firmly Dr Alan Clifford who seeks to build a major theological structure on his view that Calvin held to a universal atonement.

Robert A. Peterson Sr in his book *Calvin and the Atonement*[4] points to the fact that both sides can select evidence to support their position. Peterson observes that there are two strains in Calvin and these reflect the Bible's own antinomy between divine sovereignty and human responsibility. It is refreshing to see in Calvin's commentaries an insistence to allow the text to speak for itself even when this would seem to contradict limited atonement. Examples are John 3:16 and 1 John 2:2.

In contrast John Gill (1697-1771) in his book *The Cause of God and Truth* works on these texts in such a way to deprive them of the plain meaning they are intended to convey.

---

4   Robert A. Peterson Sr, *Calvin and the Atonement* (Tain, Ross-shire: Christian Focus Publications, 1999).

Sadly this reveals a scholastic and rationalistic way of thinking. Spurgeon in commenting on Gill's commentary describes Gill as 'hacking and hewing terribly to bring the Word of God into a more systematic shape'.[5] (John Gill will be discussed in the chapter on Hyper-Calvinism.) Arminians on the one side and Hyper-Calvinists on the other cannot live with antinomy — both impose human reasoning on the text of Scripture; both attempt to unscrew the inscrutable.

Robert A. Peterson Sr confesses, 'I have resisted the temptation to read my view into Calvin. I hold to a position of limited atonement but continue to think that the evidence is too ambiguous to allow a definitive answer to the question of what Calvin taught on the matter.'[6] Robert Letham[7] follows this view and I would also concur with this understanding of Calvin's teaching.

---

5 C. H. Spurgeon, *Commenting and Commentaries* (Grand Rapids: Kregel, 1954), 9.

6 Peterson, *Calvin and the Atonement*, 118.

7 Robert Letham, 'Saving Faith and Assurance in Reformed Theology: Zwingli to the Synod of Dort', 2 vols. (Ph.D dissertation, University of Aberdeen, 1979), 1:125-126.

6

THE EXPERIENCE OF FREE GRACE

I n times of revival sinners experience a deep conviction of their sinful condition. Sometimes this experience can be agonizing. As souls first discover their appalling condition of lostness and guilt and then are led to search for and find salvation by faith in Christ, the glory of God's grace shines resplendently. Hymns that stem from revival times express admiration and astonishment at God's saving grace. John Newton's (1725-1807) expression of gratitude is well known,

> Amazing grace! how sweet the sound
> > That saved a wretch like me!
> I once was lost, but now am found;
> > Was blind, but now I see.

The sense of former wretchedness, lostness, and blindness is replaced by an overwhelming sense of joy and praise. Likewise, that the apostle Paul should receive grace and apostleship when his activities as a persecutor warranted nothing but wrath gave him a sense of indebtedness to which he constantly testified in his preaching and letters (1 Corinthians 15:9; Galatians 1:11-24).

The experience of grace in the soul of Martin Luther was the source out of which the Lutheran Reformation was born. Luther studied under Johann von Staupitz (c.1460-1524) who was vicar-general of the Augustinian monasteries in Germany. Staupitz wished to free himself from his responsibilities, and it was obvious that he prepared Luther to be his successor. Under his spiritual guidance Luther graduated through all levels of theological study up to and including his doctorate — and this within the shortest time frame possible. Five years of study was the minimum requirement.

All this took place in spite of the fact that Luther was in spiritual turmoil. He was tormented by the fact that he had no assurance of salvation. He tried everything — including fasting and confession of all known sin. In 1513 he began lecturing on the Psalms. He went on to expound Romans and then Galatians and Hebrews. This intense study of the Scriptures was the means of his conversion. He wrestled with the meaning of the word 'righteousness' in Psalm 31 and followed that up by studying the New Testament equivalent in Romans 1:17. When he saw that God's righteousness is a free gift received by faith he was instantly liberated. He declared, 'Thereupon I felt myself to be reborn and to have gone through open doors into paradise.'[1] Luther's was a free grace experience born out of a tremendous struggle in which he came to see passionately that salvation was not by free will,

---

1 Roland Bainton, *Here I Stand* (Oxford: Lion Books, 1984), 65. Numerous editions of Bainton's book have been published.

not by works, not by religious rituals, not by confessing sins to a priest, but by grace alone.

George Whitefield (1714-1770), probably the most remarkable preacher in English church history, tells of how he came to experience free grace during a sea voyage to America as a young twenty-four-year-old. As an immensely successful preacher, the temptation to pride was as wide as the sea and sky around him because there was no preacher as eloquent as he was. Yet it was during this time that he was overcome by conviction of sin and a wretchedness so intense that he even contemplated giving up the ministry. This time of conviction, according to his own testimony, helped him to understand the doctrines of grace: election and adoption. This experience of humbling served to deepen and strengthen him and cause him to lean more upon God. This was not the last time Whitefield was to experience such conviction.[2]

After a prolonged time of deep conviction C. H. Spurgeon came to embrace free grace. He describes his experience as follows:

> Well can I remember the manner in which I learned the doctrines of grace in a single instant. Born, as all of us are by nature, an Arminian, I still believed the old things I had heard continually from the pulpit, and did not see the grace of God. When I was coming to Christ, I thought I was doing it all myself, and though I sought the Lord earnestly, I had no idea the Lord was seeking me. I do not think the young convert is at first aware of this. I can recall the very day and hour when first I received those truths in my own soul — when they were, as John Bunyan says, burnt into my heart as with a hot iron; and I can recollect how I felt that I

2 'The Doctrines of Grace' in Arnold Dallimore, *George Whitefield* (Edinburgh: The Banner of Truth Trust, 1970), vol. 1, 395-410.

had grown on a sudden from a babe into a man — that I had made progress in Scriptural knowledge, through having found once for all, the clue to the truth of God. One week-night, when I was sitting in the house of God, I was not thinking much about the preacher's sermon for I did not believe it. The thought struck me, 'How did you come to be a Christian?' I sought the Lord. 'But how did you come to seek the Lord?' The truth flashed across my mind in a moment — I should not have sought him unless there had been some previous influence in my mind to make me seek him. I prayed, thought I, but then I asked myself, How came I to pray? I was induced to pray by reading the Scriptures. How came I to read the Scriptures? I did read them, but what led me to do so? Then, in a moment, I saw that God was at the bottom of it all, and that he was the Author of my faith, and so the whole doctrine of grace opened up to me, and from that doctrine I have not departed to this day, and I desire to make this my constant confession, 'I ascribe my change wholly to God.'[3]

Turning to our day, I think of a close friend, Martin Holdt. He is a well-known pastor in South Africa. He embraced the doctrines of grace when he had been in the pastorate for little more than a year. He had been struggling with the doctrine of election. Martin was given excellent books to read in the early days when he lived in Pietersburg. His coming to the doctrines of grace was not an intellectual step only, but rather consisted of profound spiritual experience. One morning in his study he realized that just as the doctrine of the Trinity is beyond comprehension, so is the doctrine of election. When Martin embraced the doctrines of grace, peace flooded his

3   C. H. Spurgeon, *The Early Years* (Edinburgh: The Banner of Truth Trust, 1962), 164-165.

heart. He went to the kitchen to announce to his wife Beryl that he now believed the doctrine of election. She was shocked! 'What about my Dad?' she asked. Her father was a hardened unbeliever. Unpremeditated, Martin responded with the following words, 'If it is up to your Dad, you know as well as I do that he will never be converted. But if it is up to God, there is hope.' She saw that. Gradually she too came to love and to believe the doctrines of grace. Sovereign grace has been an anchor and source of strength in Martin's ministry.

The story of Drew Garner and his wife Frances illustrates the transforming power of free grace in the soul. Drew Garner was a young pastor of a large Southern Baptist church with about 1,000 members. Behind an impressive facade of highly organized and efficient evangelistic activity lay a disillusioned and theologically disorientated pastor. Drew confessed that he was far along the road of liberalism in his heart and heading straight in the direction of total scepticism and abandonment of the faith. Nevertheless the machinery had to be kept running, and the machinery of churchly activity kept him going.

One Sunday he was tipped off to visit a newcomer in the area who might, if visited, be drawn to swell the ranks of the church. Early Monday morning, Drew knocked on the door. In his own words, 'the ugliest man I have ever seen appeared unshaven and in his dressing gown'. The man informed Drew that there was time only for a few words.

'Do you make altar calls?' the ugly man growled.

'Of course I do,' said Drew.

'Why do you make them?'

'To give people a chance to decide!'

'Do you think people have to have a chance? Does God save by chance?'

Just as Drew began to think, 'What kind of a nut have I got on my hands?' the ugly man said, 'I would like you to see my library'. He showed Drew inside. A magnificent array of

Puritan books was unveiled before Drew's eyes. Although at sea theologically Drew had been well educated. He knew instinctively that he was with someone who knew what he believed, who studied those books, and who was well-grounded in Christian doctrine and life. Bringing the short meeting to a close the ugly man said, 'I want you to read two books.' He gave him Arthur Pink's *The Sovereignty of God* and Loraine Boettner's *The Reformed Doctrine of Predestination*.

Drew made a few more calls and returned home. 'A strange man called this morning on his way to work,' said Frances. 'He said he was new to the area and that he would like me to read John chapter six.' 'Was he a big ugly man?' asked Drew. 'Yes, he was' replied Frances. 'He's a nut!' said Drew, and went into his study.

As he sat down the old familiar feeling of theological desolation came upon him. He had run dry and was desperate. Apart from evangelisitic gimmickry he was doctrinally and spiritually bankrupt. His eyes fell upon the two books he had brought in. He began to read. The ugly man dropped in next day to see Frances about her progress in John 6. Her studies were going well and by Wednesday she was having a major change of mind. On Thursday Drew's reading of the two books brought him suddenly and dramatically to the point of revelation. Suddenly his eyes were opened! He saw it all in an instant! Leaping in the air he shouted as loud as it is possible for a man to shout. The whole plan of God, his sovereignty and his purpose had fallen into place. He rushed out to share it with Frances. She too had seen it. They rejoiced together. Life had begun anew. The theological desert, the barren spiritual wandering, the doubt and scepticism had all gone, and gone forever. A new life had begun.

The future years were to prove hard but rewarding. Drew Garner has never ceased to thank God for sending that excellent man and using him so decisively. In the place of evangelical tradition has come a full and rich ministry not only in the realm of soul-winning and evangelism but in pastoral work and church planting.

The blessings that result from the free grace experience are many. It is a great help to have a strong, clear grasp of God's overall plan of salvation. To be able to understand theology and rejoice in God's sovereign purpose as it is unfolded in Scripture is most helpful. As we have just seen in the case of Drew Garner, doubt was expelled. Clarity and strength of faith replaced uncertainty and doctrinal shallowness. A potent grasp of the sovereignty of God can transform a pastor's entire ministry. This was Drew Garner's experience. The change in his life is typical of those who come into deep heart experience of God's free grace.

An appreciation of the sovereignty of God in salvation results in humility. From evangelical humiliation come two essential attributes, namely, the fear of God and a humble, contrite mind. The fear of the Lord receives little if any attention in evangelical circles today. We still have the phrase, 'a God-fearing man', although it is not used as much as it used to be. The fear of God lies at the very heart of true Christianity. Both Old and New Testaments speak much of this fear. Indeed, there are hundreds of direct or indirect references to this matter in Scripture.

How does one discern a true fear of the Lord? The answer is that it is accompanied by a reverence for Scripture, a repudiation of all lightness, frivolity and flippancy, and a conformity of heart to the precepts of the Word. A true fear of the Lord is often experienced in awful stillness: 'Be still, and know that I am God' (Psalm 46:10). Such a fear leads to a thoughtful and living relationship with God in which those beautiful attributes described by our Lord in the Sermon on the Mount are developed, namely, sorrow for sin, meekness, purity, mercy, peacemaking, and joy (Matthew 5:3-12).

One of the practical effects of the fear of God is humility. The Prodigal Son was brought to humiliation. He had quickly squandered his substance and his gifts of character, thus bringing himself both to profligacy and penury. The backward slide was permitted in order to bring him to an end of himself. He showed true repentance when he determined to return to his father. That he was humbled was seen in his words, 'Father, I have sinned against heaven and in your sight, and am no longer worthy to be called your son' (Luke 15:21, NKJV). The case of the Prodigal illustrates God's purpose in the humbling of all of his people. Can you think of one saved character in Scripture who was not humbled?

Free grace causes us to abandon every reliance upon ourselves or dependence on what we have done and to look to the Lord alone to save us.

> Nothing in my hand I bring,
>   Simply to your cross I cling;
> Naked, come to you for dress,
>   Helpless, look to you for grace;
> Foul, I to the fountain fly;
>   Wash me, Saviour, or I die.[4]

Appreciation of free grace is the source of intense joy, a joy which inspires profound worship, perhaps best expressed in the hymns we sing:

> Sovereign grace o'er sin abounding,
>   Ransomed souls, the tidings swell;
> 'Tis a deep that knows no sounding;
>   Who its breadth or length can tell?

---

4   Stanza 3 of 'Rock of Ages' by Augustus Toplady (1740-1778).

On its glories
    Let my soul for ever dwell.[5]

The fruit of the experience of free grace is love, worship, gratitude, humility, joy, dedication, zeal, meekness, gentleness, and compassion towards others. Those who deeply appreciate that they have received so much so freely are the most thankful to God and the most ready to seek the good of others.

---

5 Stanza 1 of 'Sovereign grace o'er sin abounding' by John Kent (1766-1843).

7

ARMINIANISMS

The term Arminianism originated in the early seventeenth century following the Synod of Dort. The formularies of Dort clarified the issues and served the churches thereafter as guidelines to resist both Arminianism and Hyper-Calvinism. The issues debated and clarified at Dort, however, were not new.

The first great public contest over the issue of free will took place in the fourth century with Augustine (A.D. 354-430) and Pelagius (A.D. 360-420). Pelagius was a British monk who travelled and taught widely. He denied the doctrine of original sin and taught that Adam sinned only for himself. Pelagius taught that God chooses a person only because he foresees that that person will choose him.

Augustine was the most influential of the early church fathers. He firmly taught the doctrine of original sin and opposed the teachings of Pelagius. Following the tensions between Augustine and Pelagius there were those who took the middle ground (synergism) and these were called Semi-Pelagians. John Cassian (A.D. 360-435) was the leader of the Semi-Pelagians.

Gottschalk (A.D. 804-869) was a German monk who travelled extensively, teaching the five points that we now summarize in the acrostic TULIP (see chapter 4). John Wycliff (1329-1384) and John Huss (1371-1415) of Bohemia (now the Czech Republic) also affirmed the sovereignty of God in salvation.

More than any other major gathering of Christian leaders in church history, the Synod of Dort clarified the doctrines of grace. These doctrines are incorporated in the major Reformed Confessions of Faith but the formularies of Dort cover the ground in more detail.

Free will was the doctrine that characterized medieval Roman Catholicism. Martin Luther clearly expounded the central issue of free will, and his views were endorsed by other leading sixteenth-century Reformers. When challenged by the sixteenth-century Reformers, the Roman Catholic Church responded by convening the Council of Trent. Sadly the Council of Trent rejected the doctrine of justification by faith alone and at the same time endorsed Semi-Pelagianism, which is another way of describing Arminianism. In spite of the clear manifesto of Dort, Arminianism was soon widely espoused in the Anglican Church in England under the leadership of Archbishop William Laud.[1]

An early move away from the Reformed position of the

---

1   Daniel Neal, *History of the Puritans*, vol. 2, 315ff. See also H. R. Trevor-Roper, *Archbishop Laud, 1573-1645* (London: Macmillan & Co., 1962) and Nicholas Tyacke, *The Rise of English Arminianism* (Oxford: Oxford University Press, 1987).

five points as expressed by the Synod of Dort was Amyraldianism. This was a theological system developed by a French pastor Moïse Amyraut (1596-1664). Amyraut was a prolific writer. He construed that there are passages that teach that there is a universal saving will of God towards every man (2 Peter 3:9; 1 Timothy 2:4). He also maintained that some men for whom Christ died may ultimately perish (1 Corinthians 8:11; Romans 14:15; Hebrews 10:29). The development of Amyraut's thinking, and the widespread controversy resulting from his teaching, is described by Roger Nicole in a brilliant article in *The Encyclopedia of Christianity*.[2]

There are different forms of Arminianism. One distinct form is that of Wesleyan Arminianism. John Wesley (1703-1791) detested the doctrine of election. In 1739 he excommunicated a man from his Society who promoted belief in predestination, and in August of that year he published a sermon opposing unconditional election, which he entitled 'Free Grace'. That was against the advice of George Whitefield who was then across the Atlantic on his first visit to America. Throughout his ministry, John Wesley opposed implacably the doctrine of election and the perseverance of the saints. For an outstanding description of the issues involved I recommend the chapter, 'The collision with Calvinism' in Iain Murray's book *Wesley and the Men Who Followed*.[3]

Professor Tom Nettles suggests that two factors govern Wesley's exposition and polemics concerning Calvinism. The first is that 'the doctrines of grace cannot be true, because they imply reprobation. Reprobation cannot be true, because it makes God unjust. It makes God unjust because it infallibly implies that he punishes people for the commission of sins that must have been caused by his decree'.

---

2   Roger Nicole in Jay P. Green ed., *The Encyclopedia of Christianity* (1964), vol. 1.
3   Iain Murray, *Wesley and the Men Who Followed* (Edinburgh: The Banner of Truth Trust, 2003).

The second is foreknowledge. 'Foreknowledge' equals absolute and pervasive cognition of all things simultaneously. God's election arises from this and is therefore not causative of the human experience of salvation, but reflective of the eternal awareness that these experiences will happen in time.[4] In order to accommodate the idea of free grace John Wesley taught that through the Fall all men had wholly lost the power to respond to the gospel, but now that capacity to respond had been restored to every man as a gift of grace. The disciples of Arminius at the Synod of Dort maintained that free will had never been wholly lost, and 'total inability had never been a true diagnosis of man's plight in Adam'. Wesley insisted that the capacity to co-operate was itself a love-gift from God to sinners, and he agreed with the Calvinistic doctrine of original sin.[5]

A major difference between the preaching of John and Charles Wesley and most Arminians today is that the Wesleys insisted on the necessity of genuine repentance. Like John the Baptist they required fruit or evidence of repentance in practical daily living, whereas the easy believism of our day is superficial in the extreme (as illustrated in Walter Chantry's book *Today's Gospel — Authentic or Synthetic*[6]).

Various degrees of synergism characterize Arminianism. By synergism is meant the idea that God's grace is mixed with human ability. As we have just seen in the case of John Wesley, he insisted that the capacity to co-operate was itself a love-gift from God to sinners. Here is the view that God does indeed give grace to respond, but ultimately it is the will of

---

4   Tom Nettles, 'John Wesley's Contention with Calvinism: Interactions Then and Now' in T. Schreiner and B. Ware, ed., *The Grace of God and the Bondage of the Will* (Grand Rapids: Baker Books, 1995), 2:318.

5   J. I. Packer, 'Arminianisms', Puritan Conference Papers, 1968.

6   Walter Chantry, *Today's Gospel — Authentic or Synthetic?* (Edinburgh: The Banner of Truth Trust, 1985).

man that decides the issue of salvation not God alone. Synergism is the idea that we are saved by grace, but mixed with that is the merit of free will. The element of human contribution is preserved intact. I remember an evangelist debating this issue with me. He held up both hands and pointed his ten fingers towards heaven, five fingers on his left as the five points of Calvinism, and the five fingers on his right hand as the five points of Arminianism: then intertwining the fingers of his hands he proclaimed with great satisfaction that this mixture represents perfect truth! What he did illustrate was synergism! One of the purposes of the Synod of Dort was to show the impossibility, if not absurdity, of this notion, and to reject synergism.

It is true that the sinner must come voluntarily to Christ in an act of free agency. That is imperative. But according to Scripture that willingness to come to Christ and trust him wholly is in its totality attributable to the work of the Holy Spirit (Ephesians 2:1-10). Regeneration precedes repentance and faith as is seen in John 1:12-13. We receive Christ and become children of God having been 'born not of natural descent, nor of human decision or a husband's will, but born of God'. Jesus said, 'No one can come to me unless the Father who sent me draws him' (John 6:44). In that drawing there is a spiritual resurrection, a new birth, a change of nature by which the sinner becomes willing to welcome and receive the salvation that Christ offers. In that drawing there is a regeneration of the mind so that he can now see the kingdom and understand spiritual things. The natural man without this enlightenment 'does not accept the things that come from the Spirit of God, for they are foolishness to him, and he cannot understand them, because they are spiritually discerned' (1 Corinthians 2:14). Both the mind and heart are regenerated by the Holy Spirit.

In spite of the theological renewal of the last thirty to forty years in which the Reformed faith has been widely propagated, Arminianism is still common and still prevails in many evangelical circles.

THE REIGN OF ARMINIANISM IN THE USA

No survey of Arminianism up to the present time is adequate without considering the massive impact of Charles G. Finney (1792-1875). Finney was an American evangelist and leader who held the *Westminster Confession of Faith* in contempt. He denied original sin and despised the doctrine of justification by faith. He believed in the freedom of the will and held that all that was needed was the right methodology — a system of operations set in motion by human contrivance. If his methods were used, professions of faith would be multiplied. They did indeed multiply but the fall-out rate soared in proportion.

Finney's method of the altar-call became stereotyped and institutionalized in many denominations. A major part of the blame for the decline of the historic evangelical faith must be laid at the feet of Finney.[7]

Billy Sunday (1862-1935) was a famous professional baseball player. He was converted in 1886 and soon after was employed by J. Wilbur Chapman (1859-1918) who was a well-known evangelist. Chapman followed Dwight L. Moody (1837-1899) who was another very well-known American evangelist who sought to maintain high standards. Moody placed an emphasis on the 'enquiry room' where those who came forward in response to the altar-call could be counselled as to their true condition.

Billy Sunday started his own organization in 1896. He dropped the practice of the enquiry room and began to call everyone who came forward a convert. This was damaging,

---

7 Geoffrey Thomas, 'Charles Finney and Modern Evangelism' in *Reformation Today*, No.143. See also Clive Tyler, 'Finney and the Disappearance of Revival' in *Reformation Today*, No.18.

as many were told that they were Christians merely because they had come forward. It was also a snare to Billy Sunday whose reputation was inflated by the impression of thousands of converts. This practice of implying that those who respond to appeals are real converts has spread all over America — and indeed all over the world!

Billy Sunday increased the drama of his meetings by adding 'a sawdust trail' that was laid down in the aisles leading to the preacher. Sunday used his celebrity status as a former baseball player to add attraction to coming forward at the end of the sermon. Thus, there were mixed motives for his hearers to come walking down the sawdust trails to the front and shake his hand. Billy Sunday would exclaim, 'How many of you will settle the great question without the delay of another minute, by coming forward to take me by the hand and by doing so confess and accept Jesus Christ as your personal Saviour? Will you come?'

This conveyed the notion that the physical act of walking the sawdust trail was an act of saving faith. This is a typical press report: 'Converts rushed to grasp the hand of Billy Sunday. 425 men, women and children of all ages and types surged down the sawdust trail to the platform at the tabernacle last night to grasp the hand of Billy Sunday and to be enrolled as professing Christians.'

Sunday used every pretext available to persuade people to hit the sawdust trail. If people from Scotland were present he would remind them that Scottish people are renowned for their courage. He would appeal to railroad workers and wave a green lantern. To a Swedish delegation one night he shouted. 'Come on, Swedes! The Swedes have never been cowards yet! So come on!'[8]

---

8 Patrick McIntyre, *The Graham Formula: Why Most Decisions for Christ are Ineffective* (Mamoth Spring, AR: White Harvest Publishing, 2006).

At one time he used a three-fold challenge, 'If you are against booze, and you are for America, and you are for Jesus, then come and shake my hand.' Sometimes the stream coming down the sawdust trail was so great that there would be two lines, one to shake his left hand and the other to shake his right hand.

Billy Sunday's music director for seventeen years, Homer Rodeheaver (1880-1955), eventually resigned, pointing out the dishonesty of these methods. It was clear that the biblical doctrine of sin was missing in this kind of evangelism.

There was a widespread perception that the Billy Sunday practice was superficial and that it takes far more than shaking the evangelist's hand or repeating a penitential prayer to becoming a real, born-again Christian. G. Campbell Morgan (1863-1945), who preceded Dr Martyn Lloyd-Jones (1899-1981) at Westminster Chapel in London, England, was a contemporary of Billy Sunday. Morgan affirmed his belief in the necessity of careful and diligent counselling. Although Arminian himself, Campbell Morgan was sceptical of the inflated claims made using the Billy Sunday methods.[9]

The altar-call methodology is thoroughly Arminian. It is in stark contrast to the preaching of John the Baptist who was not flattered by the Pharisees who came to hear him. He called them snakes and demanded of them evidence to prove their repentance. When the rich young ruler came running to Jesus to ask for eternal life, Jesus gave no indication of an easy way, no signing of a decision card. Rather, he probed his motives and told him to go home and sell everything that he had and give the money to the poor, and then come and take up discipleship. If altar-call evangelists followed that searching policy it would end their altar-call practice forthwith.

These shallow methods and shortcuts stem from the idea that conversion can be achieved by a decision. This is raw

---

9   McIntyre, *The Graham Formula*, 48.

Arminianism. Millions in America who show no signs of regeneration believe that they are saved because they have responded at one time or another to an appeal. That is why I have used the heading above: 'The reign of Arminianism in the USA'. Millions have signed a card or made a decision; some have responded many times. If every recorded decision were counted as a genuine conversion, then there are more Christians in America than there are people! In the Southern Baptist Convention (the largest Protestant denomination in the USA), the altar-call is tantamount to a sacrament like baptism and the Lord's Table. If a minister does not employ this method of calling people to the front at the end of each service he is regarded as less than evangelical. Professor Tom Nettles told me that when he was a boy he responded to the altar-call every week. One day his father said to him, 'Son, you do not have to go forward *every* week!'

The result of this practice is that there are many churches with substantial memberships, consisting largely of people who do not attend services, still less the prayer meetings. A typical example would be 1,000 members with 700 to 800 rarely seen, and hundreds who haven't been seen at church for years. If moves are taken to purge the membership of those who are obviously only nominal, there is an outcry and the pastor is in danger of being fired.

The idea that using the altar-call produces converts is injurious. Think of a preacher going home with the satisfaction that five converts have been made because five came to the front in response to his altar-call. In one year there might be about 200 such responses but not one lasting conversion. It sounds so good for a preacher to be able to report that people responded to his appeal, and it gives the impression that they are all converts. This is deceptive.

I attended an American Baptist church where the visiting preacher made an altar-call at the end of his very poor sermon.

The congregation consisted of about 120 souls. No one responded. Obviously wishing to save face he then called for those who wished to rededicate their lives to Christ to come forward. He cajoled the people for a while but no one moved. He then called for those who wanted to be healed to come forward. An elderly, frail couple moved to the front. I learned afterward that this couple are in bad health and readily respond to a call for prayer. However, the overall impression of that service was distasteful. The attempt to manipulate the congregation was repugnant.

Steps to correct the shortfalls in altar-call evangelism have been taken by the Billy Graham organization. Their emphasis is threefold: 1. Excellent preaching, 2. Counselling after the altar-call, and 3. Intensive follow-up by counsellors and churches thereafter. However, the ecumenical policy they use, points to the inherent deficiency of the system. Those counselled are recommended to Roman Catholic or liberal churches if those are the churches from which they have been directed to the crusade. To cite one example: of over 1,300 Catholics who came forward at a San Francisco Crusade, practically all remained Catholic, continued to pray to Mary, went to Mass, and confessed to their priests.[10]

The idea that follow-up can make up for the failure of decisionism is addressed by Pastor Jim Elliff:

> A great mistake is made by blaming the problem on poor follow-up. In many churches there is every intention and effort given to follow-up, yet still the poor numbers persist. One church followed up 'by the book', seeking to disciple people who had been told they were new converts during the crusade of an internationally known evangelist. The report of the pastor in

---

10 Erroll Hulse, *Billy Graham, The Pastor's Dilemma* (Maurice Allan Ltd, 1969), 44. This book is no longer in print.

charge was that none of them wanted to talk about how to grow as a Christian. He said, 'In fact, they ran from us!' I have known some churches to go to extreme efforts to disciple new believers. We must do this. Yet, like the others, they generally have marginal success. They have learned to accept the fact that people who profess to have become Christians often have to be talked into going further, and that many, if not most, simply will not bother. Authentic new believers can *always* be followed up, however, because they have the Spirit by which they cry, 'Abba, Father' (Romans 8:15). They have been given love for the brethren, and essential love for the beauty and authority of the Word of God. But you *cannot* follow up on a spiritually dead person. Being dead, he has no interest in growth.[11]

The pitfalls of the invitation system are illustrated by the experience of Dawson Trotman (1906-1956) who founded the organization called The Navigators. Trotman made a typical decision for Christ at age fourteen in 1920 and joined a Presbyterian church. However there was no change in his sinful lifestyle — he continued to lie, steal, get drunk, and use profane language. In 1926 he experienced true conversion and the power of the Holy Spirit to live a godly life. He then witnessed to everyone he met and specialized in giving lifts to hitchhikers. He claimed that everyone he picked up he persuaded to accept Christ. He then began to detect that there was no change in the lives of those he believed he had led to Christ. Trotman did not embrace the Reformed faith but he did institute methods in his organization designed to disciple those who made a profession of faith.

---

11 Jim Elliff, 'Southern Baptists, an Unregenerate Denomination'. See www.ccwonline.org/sbc.html.

Ultimately it takes persevering personal friendship and discipling to establish those who show interest in the gospel. Often it takes years before a believer is truly established in the faith. The reality of the supernatural nature of the new birth is illustrated in the lives of drug addicts and alcoholics. An addict can make a decision in meetings a hundred times but until the Holy Spirit works in power there will be no mortification of sin and no change in his enslaved lifestyle.

To what extent does the Holy Spirit work within the invitation system? In my book *The Great Invitation* I outline the history, development, and features of the invitation system. I describe famous preachers who never used the invitation system and discuss reasons for and against using the altar-call.[12] A few are saved through the preaching and others through the process of counselling that follows, not merely after the meeting, but in the weeks and months afterwards. The proportion of those lastingly converted is small. In the days of Billy Sunday, the saying was common in reference to his work: 'two dollars a soul'. In other words the professions made did not add up to very much if it cost the Billy Sunday organization only two dollars per soul to come down the sawdust trail. By omitting heart repentance, going forward is rendered meaningless. There is such a thing as notional faith, which assents to truths but does not act on them.[13]

Bill Bright (1921-2003), the founder of Campus Crusade for Christ, was another major propagator of decisionism. Bright's approach was to encourage those who have made decisions not to go by their feelings if there is no change in their lives. As an evangelist Bill Bright made it so easy to accept Christ that 80,000 out of 100,000 at one of his meetings in

---

12 Erroll Hulse, *The Great Invitation* (Laurel, MS: Audubon Press, 2006).

13 Pastor Jim Elliff helpfully explains different ways in which faith can fall short of saving faith in his booklet, *Wasted Faith* (Christian Communicators Worldwide, 1995), www.ccwonline.org.

Russia prayed the salvation prayer. In 1988, in Sudan, there were almost a million decisions for Christ.[14] Bill Bright's attitude was to hand over to the Holy Spirit responsibility for the future of those who have made a decision — that is ludicrous! Imagine a pastor saying that he is not going to shepherd the flock because the Holy Spirit will do it! This policy has contributed to the idea that you can be saved by making a decision for Christ as your Saviour, and later when you believe on Jesus as Lord you gain your sanctification. This two-tier system is a deception, because Jesus disowns those who refuse to obey him (Matthew 10:37-39). It is those who build their house on the rock who will stand in the Judgement (Matthew 7:24-29). We have returned to the fact that without holiness no one will see the Lord (Hebrews 12:14).

The American Southern Presbyterian theologian Robert Lewis Dabney (1820-1898) was perceptive in his analysis of the disillusionment of people who have been counselled because of a decision. He wrote:

> Some of these individuals feel that a cruel trick has been played upon their inexperience by the ministers and friends of Christianity in thus thrusting them, in the hour of their confusion, into false positions, whose duties they do not and cannot perform, and into sacred professions which they have been compelled shamefully to repudiate. Their self-respect is therefore galled to the quick, and pride is indignant at the humiliating exposure. No wonder that they look on religion and its advocates henceforward with suspicion and anger. They are conscious that they were thoroughly in earnest in their religious anxieties and resolves at the time, and that they felt strange and profound exercises. Yet bitter

---

14 McIntyre, *The Graham Formula*, 60.

and mortifying experience has taught them that their new birth and experimental religion at least was a delusion. How natural to conclude that those of all others are delusions also. They say: 'the only difference between myself and these earnest Christians is, that they have not yet detected the cheat as I have. They are now not a whit more convinced of their sincerity and of the reality of their exercises than I once was of mine. Yet I know there was no change in my soul; I do not believe that there is in theirs.' Such is the fatal process of thought through which thousands have passed; until the country is sprinkled all over with infidels, who have been made such by their own experience of spurious religious excitements. They may keep their hostility to themselves in the main; because Christianity now 'walks in her silver slippers'; but they are not the less steeled against all saving impressions of the truth.[15]

How long will Arminianism reign in the USA and dominate in evangelical circles in many other countries? My reading of the situation is that as liberal theology has declined since the 1960s, so Arminianism is on the wane. Arminianism does not thrive where there is systematic expository preaching. There are excellent Presbyterian and Baptist seminaries in the USA where the doctrines of grace are taught — that is a hopeful sign for the future.

---

15 R. L. Dabney, *Discussions*, vol. 1, 572. See also vol. 2, 654-655.

8

THE GOLDEN CHAIN

Within the context of administering comfort to the suffering people of God in Romans 8, verse 28 marks a turning point. Having described life in the Spirit, the apostle Paul introduces the purpose of God our Father: 'And we know that all things work together for good to those who love God, to those who are the called according to his purpose' (NKJV). This purpose of the Father is then described by way of *five actions* which are joined together like links in a chain, sometimes called 'the golden chain'. Paul writes, 'For those God foreknew he also predestined to be conformed to the likeness of his Son, that he might be the firstborn among many brothers. And those he predestined, he also called; those he called, he also justified; those he justified, he also glorified' (Romans 8:29-30).

Arminians base their view of salvation on the idea that God foresees those who believe and that is what makes the difference between the saved and the unsaved. It is vital therefore that we view foreknowledge in the context of the Father's gracious actions. Each of the five actions of God is in the aorist. The aorist tense in Greek denotes an action or an event. Its function is not one primarily concerned with time but rather with drawing attention to the significance of that action or event. The stress therefore in these five actions is on the significance of each action as an event.

These are the five actions of God the Father:

1. He loved us.
2. He predestined us.
3. He called us.
4. He justified us.
5. He glorified us.

The initiative in each of these actions is ascribed to the Father. The purpose of each action is for our good. These actions are sovereign in the sense that God is active and we are passive. They are gracious actions because as sinners and rebels we deserve nothing.

1. HE LOVED US

The text declares, 'For whom he foreknew'. Of course God knows all things and he knows everyone in the universal sense. Here a specific people are in view, not events and certainly not faith foreseen. Merely to know about is not an action. To possess knowledge about someone is not an action. In his commentary on Romans, Professor John Murray writes: 'Many times in Scripture "know" has a pregnant meaning which goes beyond that of mere cognition. It is used in a sense practically synonymous with "love", to set regard upon, to know with peculiar interest, delight, and action.'[1]

The Hebraic meaning of foreknowledge is implicit in New Testament usage. It is the idea of an intimate relationship. 'To know' refers to covenantal love. The meaning of intimate knowledge is conveyed by Amos 3:2: 'You only have I known of all the families of the earth' (NKJV). Also Hosea uses the term 'to know' to refer to a marriage relationship: 'I knew you in the wilderness, in the land of great drought' (Hosea 13:5, NKJV). In that terrible experience in the wilderness, Jehovah was joined to his people. The verb *jada*, love, often carries considerable depth of meaning in the Old Testament conveying the idea of a deep relationship of love. The Lord said to Jeremiah, 'Before I formed you in the womb I knew you, before you were born I set you apart' (Jeremiah 1:5). There is a lament when this kind of knowledge of love is absent (Hosea 4:1; 6:6).

This fact of love is expressed in 1 Peter 1:20 where Christ is described as foreknown: 'For he was foreknown before the foundation of the world, but has appeared in these last times for the sake of you' (NASB). The NIV translates it as: 'He was chosen before the creation of the world'. Peter speaks of God's foreknowledge of Christ in terms of choosing and appointing him to be our Redeemer. In the introduction Peter describes the elect as those 'who have been chosen according to the foreknowledge of God the Father' (1 Peter 1:2). In other words they are beloved of God the Father. 'To know' means to know intimately. Jesus says, 'I know my sheep and my sheep know me' (John 10:14). Thus Paul strongly rejects the idea that the Lord has cast away a people that 'he foreknew' (Romans 11:2). That does not mean a people whom he merely knew about — it means a people upon whom *he set his love*.

---

1 John Murray, *The Epistle to the Romans* (Grand Rapids: Eerdmans, 1997).

'Foreknow' focuses attention upon the distinguishing love of God whereby the children of God were elected. In this way we understand Paul when he declares of the Father, 'he chose us in him before the creation of the world to be holy and blameless in his sight' (Ephesians 1:4). The next action is predestination: 'In love he predestined us to be adopted as his sons through Jesus Christ' (Ephesians 1:5). The grace given to us has its spring in the love of God the Father (2 Thessalonians 2:16). The Father has given a people to Christ (John 6:37). Christ's love for his people is concurrent with that of his Father. It is this love that sustained Christ in his determination to go through with the crucifixion (Romans 5:6-8; 8:37; Galatians 2:20; Hebrews 12:2).

This truth is practical. The context of Romans 8:18 concerns our present sufferings. We are comforted by the knowledge of the eternal electing love of God and that we are chosen to be in Christ. That love is a superlative love! It is the 'so loved'. The Father *so loved* that he gave his one and only Son to be the propitiation for our sins. How can we respond to this great love? The answer: 'Beloved, if God so loved us, we also ought to love one another' (1 John 4:11, NASB).

2. HE PREDESTINED US

Paul writes to the Ephesians, 'In him we were also chosen, having been predestined according to the plan of him who works out everything in conformity with the purpose of his will' (Ephesians 1:11). The love of God the Father is active and this is the source of his foreordination of his people to eternal life. Here, predestination focuses on God's people and, in particular, the purpose that they should be conformed to the likeness of Christ, 'that he might be the firstborn among many brothers' (Romans 8:29). The term 'firstborn' reflects the priority and supremacy of Christ (Colossians 1:15-18; Hebrews 1:6; Revelation 1:5).

Predestination means that,

> From all eternity God decreed all that should happen
> in time, and this he did freely and unalterably, consult-
> ing only his own wise and holy will. Yet in so doing
> he does not become in any sense the author of sin,
> nor does he share responsibility for sin with sinners.
> Neither, by reason of his decree, is the will of any crea-
> ture he has made violated; nor is the free working of
> second causes put aside; rather it is established.[2]

Predestination points to the origin of all things while providence points to the direct control of the Holy Spirit over all
things in creation and in human affairs. To cite the *1689
Confession*: 'Nothing happens by chance or outside the sphere
of God's providence. As God is the first cause of all events,
they happen immutably and infallibly according to his foreknowledge and decree, to which they stand related'.[3] Thus
Peter reminds his hearers at Pentecost that Christ suffered
according to 'the set purpose and foreknowledge of God' (Acts
2:23). The control of the Spirit in providence is not merely
general. It is particular even to a sparrow's life and the hair
upon our heads (Matthew 10:29-30).

The predestination of the Father is the second action in the
five and is the only one that is elaborated further. The great
end of the Father's purpose is our sanctification: 'He predestined us to be conformed to the image of his Son that he
might be the firstborn among many brethren' (Romans 8:29).
We should note that this is intensely practical. Conformity to
the likeness of Christ involves progressive sanctification, which
is every Christian's business every hour of every day (Romans

---

2 Chapter 3, Paragraph 1, in *A Faith to Confess: The Baptist Confession of 1689*
(Sussex: Carey Publications, 1975), 20.

3 Chapter 5, Paragraph 2, in *A Faith to Confess*, 23.

12:1; 2 Corinthians 3:18; Philippians 2:12-13). The end of the process will be glorification when we will be like Christ who is our prototype (Philippians 3:21). Our glory is to share his glory (2 Corinthians 3:18; 1 John 3:2). Yet he has a *unique glory* (Hebrews 1:6). We look forward to the full expression and enjoyment of our adoption as his brothers (Hebrews 2:10-18). We anticipate the glorification described in Revelation 21:2, the glorification of Christ's redeemed people who will then be perfected and be perfectly holy, just as he is perfectly holy. This reality is expressed in Hebrews 2:13: 'Here am I, and the children God has given me'.

This truth is comforting for it shows that everything is under the complete control of God: 'Known to God from eternity are all his works' (Acts 15:18, NKJV). He knows what is to come for he has decreed what is to come.

God's absolute sovereignty is a great spiritual strength to us. We are in conflict with the post-modern philosophical climate of today in which nothing is regarded as sure. We must proclaim boldly the absolute sovereignty of the God of the Bible in everything. Western culture is similar to that of Athens when Paul preached at Mars Hill and asserted, 'For in him we live and move and have our being' (Acts 17:28). We must not be discouraged by the indifference and unbelief of the unregenerate mindset that surrounds us, but be encouraged by the promise that the Holy Spirit will convince our hearers of sin, righteousness, and judgement to come (John 16:8).

3. HE CALLED US

In the opening sentence of the letter to the Romans Paul describes himself as called to be an apostle and then describes the believers in Rome as 'those who are called to belong to Jesus Christ' and 'those called to be saints'. The Father who has loved us and predestined us is the Author of our calling. This calling is an act and not a process.

Note the explicit role of the Father when Paul declares, 'God, who has called you into fellowship with his Son Jesus Christ our Lord, is faithful' (1 Corinthians 1:9). This calling is described in Paul's second letter to Timothy: 'God who has saved us and called us to a holy life — not because of anything we have done but because of his own purpose and grace. This grace was given us in Christ Jesus before the beginning of time' (2 Timothy 1:9).

We are to declare the praises of our Father who has effectually called us with a high (Philippians 3:14), heavenly (Hebrews 3:1), and holy (2 Timothy 1:9) calling. We are to give diligence to make this calling sure (2 Peter 1:10). This calling from our Father is a calling to peace (Colossians 3:15). It is a calling to patience which endures beatings: 'But how is it to your credit if you receive a beating for doing wrong and endure it? But if you suffer for doing good and you endure it, this is commendable before God. To this you were called' (1 Peter 2:20-21).

4. HE JUSTIFIED US

Justification by faith is the central theme of Romans. Having introduced this in Romans 1:16-17 the apostle Paul goes on to show that the world, Jewish and Gentile, is destitute of righteousness. But now a saving righteousness is provided through the redemption that is in Christ (Romans 3:21-26). The method of justification he shows to be the same in all ages, namely by faith alone (Romans 4). The blessings that accrue are described in Romans 5. In Romans 6 and 7 the relationship of justification to sanctification is expounded.

The *Westminster Shorter Catechism* aptly summarizes this teaching when it describes justification as an 'act of God's free grace, wherein he freely pardons all our sins, and accepts us as righteous in his sight, only for the righteousness of Christ imputed to us, which is received by faith alone'.

'Imputation' is a theological term that will help us understand the doctrine of justification. The dictionary defines imputation as meaning, 'to ascribe', or 'to reckon'. For God to justify us he imputed Christ's righteousness to us by attributing the benefit of his work to our lives. In doing that, God declares the sinful man or woman to be righteous in his sight. The doctrine of justification means that before the eyes of God the sinful man or woman is now 'in Christ' and has perfectly kept the law of God. We can even say that 'in Christ' we have loved the Lord our God with all our heart, soul, mind, and strength and our neighbour as ourselves. This means that we look to Christ and to his living and dying for us as 'our righteousness' — no other righteousness will do! Our human efforts to keep the law or to please God fall hopelessly short. We cannot place our trust in our Christian service, our worship services, or even our religious experiences. It is pointless to trust in our religious background or what others think of us. The righteousness we need comes from *outside* of us and must be imputed to us. So we look to Christ who has power to pardon all our sins and accept us as righteous in his sight. The greater our understanding of this central truth of the Christian faith, the more intense will be our love for Christ and his free grace.[4]

Justification is a marvel. Why? God does what a human judge cannot and must not do. He declares righteous those who are sinful. If human magistrates did this it would be an abomination (Proverbs 17:15). Yet our omnipotent Creator does it and is righteous in doing so. In fact the bottom line is justice — that he might be just and the justifier of him who believes in Jesus (Romans 3:26). The Father's justification is not as scandalous as it first appears because it is based on our union with Christ. That union supplies the righteousness

---

4   This paragraph is cited from a manuscript yet to be published on the *Westminster Shorter Catechism* by Dennis Hustedt.

which is the only ground of justification — that is forensic and external. At the same time our union with Christ supplies rivers of living water, life abundant, in our hearts, and that is internal.

Justification is the foundation of our assurance. When condemned by devils or by our own conscience we take refuge in justification: 'Who will bring any charge against those whom God has chosen? It is God who justifies!' (Romans 8:33). We claim this justification in the context of union with Christ and the pursuit of holiness (Romans 6:1-4; 2 Corinthians 7:1).

5. HE GLORIFIED US

Glorification is the final step in the application of redemption. In line with the previous acts, this too is attributed to the Father. It will take place when Christ returns. At his command the bodies of all believers from all time will be raised and reunited with their souls. Every believer will then have a perfect resurrection body like that of Christ himself. The Holy Spirit will be the immediate agent of omnipotent power to achieve this, the greatest of all recreative miracles. Yet, while there is concurrence in the Trinity, this glorification of believers is specified as the act of God the Father, thereby affirming that this is his ultimate will for those who are members of his family by adoption.

Sometimes readers wonder why glorification is expressed in a past tense. We noted at the beginning that the aorist tense denotes an action or an event. Its function is not one primarily concerned with time but rather with drawing attention to the significance of an action or event. That action or event is being highlighted in its entirety. The stress therefore in these five actions is on the significance of each action as an event.

This glorification means that our bodies will be redeemed. The most detailed description of what this will involve is

1 Corinthians 15:35-58, in which the words most striking are 'powerful' and 'imperishable'. These are telling adjectives which relate to our resurrected bodies.

The glorification which all the redeemed will experience together must be related to the intermediate state. At death, our souls are 'made perfect in holiness, and do immediately pass into glory; and [our] bodies, being still united to Christ, do rest in their graves until the resurrection'.[5] When a believer dies he is absent from his body and his soul is present with the Lord (2 Corinthians 5:8); that state is described in Hebrews 12:22-24. That is a glorious company and a wonderful state! However it precedes that final glorious realm to be ushered in when our Lord returns and until that time we eagerly await the redemption of our bodies (Romans 8:23).

When our bodies are raised from the dead and our souls are re-united with our bodies we will experience complete victory over death. Death will be swallowed up in victory (1 Corinthians 15:54). This victory will be overwhelming and comprehensive. It will extend to the whole creation: 'The creation itself will be liberated from its bondage to decay and brought into the glorious freedom of the children of God' (Romans 8:21). As Adam and Eve were placed in a habitat or environment suited to them, so we will be. The earth will be a glorified earth. Today as never before cameras explore the exquisite glories of this present creation: trees, flowers, marine life, and animals. If Christians were producing these shows, appropriate psalms and hymns would be included, ascribing the praise to our Creator.

We must depict heaven as a new earth, not skies. Some hymns convey the idea that we will be eternal astronauts fixed in orbit. Little wonder that some deride that as boring. We need a better term than 'heaven', because that conveys the

---

5 The *Westminster Shorter Catechism*, Question 37.

idea of skies. The glorification of the body means that we will not be spirits forever sailing in the skies. Just as it is heresy to suggest that Christ's resurrection was merely spiritual and not physical, so it is heretical and harmful to promote the idea that in the next world we will be mere spirits. Any view which deprives us of our intrinsic and essential humanity and which radically disconnects us from a human environment is wrong. The truth is that we will be as we are now, but free entirely from sin, disease, and the ageing process. Our minds and bodies will possess additional capacities and those lacks which frustrate and torment us now will be repaired and made good.

With regard to our glorification we have to balance what we do know with what is too advanced for us at this stage, as the Scripture says, 'No eye has seen, no ear has heard, no mind has conceived what God has prepared for those who love him' (1 Corinthians 2:9). At the same time Paul prays that we might know the hope to which we have been called and the riches of our inheritance (Ephesians 1:18).

Meditation on the certainty and reality of our glorification as an act of God the Father is encouraged by Paul. He reminds us that we are gradually dying but we look forward to a powerful body which can never die, a body which in the analogy of construction is like a stone building compared with a canvas tent (2 Corinthians 4:16 – 5:5).

Romans 8:28-30 shows that salvation is by grace alone. Salvation has its inception in the love of the Father. This love is expressed in the gift of Christ and in Christ's own love for us. Nothing can sever us from that love. With confidence then we can say that we are more than conquerors through him who loved us!

9

THE DANGER OF HYPER-CALVINISM

T he formularies of Dort were sensitive to the issues in which Calvinism can be misrepresented. It is vital to know the difference between Calvinism and Hyper-Calvinism since it is common for those who are exposed to Calvinism for the first time to label Calvinists as Hyper-Calvinists.

WHAT IS HYPER-CALVINISM?

Hyper-Calvinism denies both the free offer of the gospel and common grace.[1] In essence, Hyper-Calvinists would emphasize

---

1 For example, Herman Hanko and Homer Hoeksema prove the five points but then go on to affirm classic Hyper-Calvinism [*The Five Points of Calvinism* (Grand Rapids: Reformed Free Publishing Association, 1976)].

divine responsibility to the exclusion of human responsibility. Since Calvinists believe that the work of salvation is entirely God's work, Hyper-Calvinists would take that a step further and say that since men and women can do nothing to save themselves, it is wrong to call people to do what they cannot do — it is just for God to work in the heart, not for others to call them to repentance. For example, in Articles 32 to 34 of the Gospel Standard denomination in the UK, it says that it is wrong for ministers to call on unregenerate people to savingly repent, believe, and receive Christ, because that implies that they have the power to perform those acts.[2]

The history of Hyper-Calvinism in England can be traced back to Joseph Hussey (1659-1726). Hussey was a Congregationalist evangelist who came to deny the free offers of the gospel. Subsequently, he wrote a definitive treatise with the title *God's Operation of Grace But No Offers of Grace* (1707). John Skepp, one of Hussey's disciples, further explained this view of the special work of the Holy Spirit, which precludes giving the free offer of the gospel, as did another author, John Brine. Also in this circle was John Gill whose Hyper-Calvinist influence extended across Baptist denominations in both Britain and America over the ensuing generations.

THE INFLUENCE OF JOHN GILL

John Gill was one of the long line of ministers of the Baptist church in Southwark which was eventually to have C. H. Spurgeon as pastor. Benjamin Keach (1640-1704) was its first pastor — exercising his ministry there for thirty-six years. Keach was followed by his son-in-law Benjamin Stinton who died in 1718 after just fourteen years of ministry. John Gill, aged only twenty-one, followed, pastoring there for over fifty-one years. Murdina MacDonald's research suggests that from 90 members

---

2   See Bernard Honeysett, 'The Ill-fated Articles', *Reformation Today*, Issue 2.

in 1719 the membership rose to 151 by the end of 1727. There was a move to Carter Lane in 1757 when the membership was 141. In the last two years of his ministry, Gill, on account of ill-health, could only preach once on the Lord's Day. When he died in 1771 the membership was about 133. John Rippon (1751-1836) followed even though many objected that at twenty he was far too young. He laboured from 1773 to 1836, an amazing sixty-three years — it seems that pastors seldom retired in those days! Sadly Rippon outlived his usefulness. Three lesser known men of different capacities followed, and when Spurgeon was installed as pastor in 1854 the membership was low.

But we return now to John Gill. Gill was an immensely learned Hebrew scholar. In addition to his preaching and pastoral commitments Gill was a prodigious author. His writing career began with an exposition of the Song of Solomon published in 1728. By 1729 a circle of friends were so impressed with Gill that they sponsored him to give a weekly Wednesday lecture, which he fulfilled for twenty-seven years. This became the springboard for his written ministry, which included four volumes called *The Cause of God and Truth*, which has to be read with caution. Spurgeon in his *Commenting and Commentaries* says of Gill's commentaries that when he falls on a text which is not congenial with his creed he 'hacks and hews terribly' to bring the Word of God into a more systematic shape.

John Gill was the first commentator to complete a commentary on the whole Bible. The Puritan commentators Matthew Henry (1662-1714) and Matthew Poole (1624-1679) died before they completed theirs. Gill also wrote *A Complete Body of Divinity* noted for its clarity and usefulness. These writings served to earn Gill high esteem. However this was a mixed blessing, because Hyper-Calvinism was re-inforced by Gill's constricted exegesis of biblical texts that promote the freeness of gospel invitations. Overall assessment of Gill's influence is difficult because he was used of God to give doctrinal stability to the Baptists during a time of theological weakness. My view of Gill has been affected by the negative effects I have witnessed in churches that espouse his doctrinal stance against the free offer of the gospel. For an overall balanced view of Gill, I recommend Robert Oliver in his writing on Gill in the volume *The British Particular Baptists*,[3] and his book *History of the English Calvinistic Baptists 1771-1892*, where he begins his treatise with a chapter entitled 'The legacy of John Gill'.[4]

John Gill taught the eternal justification of the elect, which is condemned in the confessions of the seventeenth century. This points us to the essence of Hyper-Calvinism which is thinking in terms of the secret will of God and seeking to read those decrees in the process of time: 'The secret things belong to the LORD our God, but the things revealed belong to us and to our sons forever, that we may observe all the words of this law' (Deuteronomy 29:29, NASB). God deals with people in time as responsible agents. For instance, we see this in the life of King Saul. Saul started well but veered off track and incurred God's displeasure. Anyone reading his life story for the first time would not know the ultimate outcome. God deals with us moment by moment, and the enjoyment of his love of delight is conditional on our obedience to his commandments (Deuteronomy 30:9-10).

At the church in Southwark, Gill replaced *Keach's Confession* (1696), which was largely based on the *Second London Baptist Confession of Faith of 1689*, and adopted a confession of faith

---

3 Robert W. Oliver in Michael A. G Haykin, ed., *The British Particular Baptists, 1638-1930* (Springfield: Particular Baptist Press, 1998). See also Robert Oliver in Michael A. G. Haykin, ed., *The Life and Thought of John Gill (1697-1771): A Tercentennial Appreciation* (Boston: Brill, 1997).

4 Robert W. Oliver, *History of the English Calvinistic Baptists, 1771-1892* (Edinburgh: The Banner of Truth Trust, 2006).

that he had prepared. Others followed this pattern, and it furthered the decline of many Baptist churches into Hyper-Calvinism right up to the time when Andrew Fuller (1754-1815) and others were involved in a mighty battle to get English Baptists back to biblical Calvinism and missionary vision and zeal.

ANDREW FULLER REFUTES HYPER-CALVINISM

Andrew Fuller was born into and grew up in the ethos of Hyper-Calvinism. It was in this atmosphere that the Lord prepared him to be the deliverer of his people and to be a leader in the Great Missionary Awakening in which William Carey (1761-1834) was a pioneer missionary. The son of a Cambridge farmer, Fuller was of powerful build and was a wrestler in his youth. He was ordained as minister of Soham Baptist Church in 1775 and inducted to the Kettering church in 1783. In his studies of theology, he was inspired and influenced by Jonathan Edwards (1703-1758). It was in 1784 that Andrew Fuller published his book *The Gospel Worthy of All Acceptation*, which launched him into a sea of controversy. To this day the name of Fuller is disparaged by Hyper-Calvinists.

How did Fuller proceed in his refutation of Hyper-Calvinism? In part one he asserts that it is the duty of all who hear the gospel to believe in Christ with such a faith as issues in salvation. What is this saving faith? It is such a faith that trusts in Christ (Mark 16:15-16; John 20:31).

Part two develops this further and consists of arguments to prove that faith in Christ is the duty of all who hear the gospel. Fuller's headings are:

1. Unconverted sinners are commanded, exhorted, and invited to believe in Christ for salvation. Here John 12:36 is cited: 'While ye have light, believe in the light, that ye may be the children of light' (KJV). He also

quotes John 6:29, Psalm 2:11-12, and Jeremiah 6:10,16 to prove his point.

2. The gospel also requires obedience, and such obedience as includes saving faith (Romans 1:5). Here he refers to 2 Thessalonians 1:8-9. Not to obey the gospel is a heinous sin.

3. Scripture ascribes the want of faith in Christ to men's depravity.

4. God has threatened and inflicted the most awful punishments on sinners for their not believing on the Lord Jesus Christ.

In part three Fuller answers objections and affirms his faith in particular redemption, and in fact covers ground very similar to the formularies of Dort. In his concluding applications, Fuller asserts his faith in the fact that God has ordained the free and solemn addresses, invitations, calls, and warnings to be *the very means ordained by God* to bring sinners to Christ.

SPURGEON'S RESPONSE TO HYPER-CALVINISM

If the battles that raged around Andrew Fuller formed the first major doctrinal conflict with Hyper-Calvinism, the second major time of controversy involved C. H. Spurgeon.[5] When Spurgeon arrived in London in 1854 the leading Baptist preacher in South London was James Wells (1803-1872), an avowed Hyper-Calvinist. Wells was a self-educated man of outstanding abilities and exceptional energy. He pastored the Surrey Tabernacle — which had twice to be enlarged to contain a regular congregation of 1,200.

Another important figure at this time was Charles Waters Banks (1806-1886). He was a minister and the editor of a

---

5   Iain Murray, *Spurgeon versus Hyper-Calvinism — The Battle for Gospel Preaching* (Edinburgh: The Banner of Truth Trust, 1995). This book expounds the universal gospel invitations, the warrant of faith, human responsibility, and the love of God.

magazine called *Earthen Vessel*, which he edited for forty-three years. Banks sought to encourage the young Spurgeon, and this did not please the above-mentioned James Wells. Wells was strongly opposed to what he regarded as Spurgeon's 'Fullerism'. So Banks was caught between the two.

Spurgeon's theology is the theology of the English Puritans: 'I have all the Puritans with me — the whole of them without a single exception.'[6] It was from the Puritans that he derived his materials. He declared,

> The doctrine I preach is that of the Puritans; it is the doctrine of Calvin, the doctrine of Augustine, the doctrine of Paul, the doctrine of the Holy Ghost. The Author and Finisher of our faith himself taught most blessed truth which well agreed with Paul's declaration, 'By grace are ye saved.' The doctrine of grace is the substance of the testimony of Jesus.[7]

So how did Spurgeon respond to Hyper-Calvinism? First, he followed Fuller in maintaining that the gospel invitations are to be universally applied. Hyper-Calvinists hold that invitations are only for 'sensible sinners' who have a felt need. 'Sensible' in those days meant sensitively aware. Spurgeon rejected this restriction.

Second, Spurgeon affirmed what we call the *objective warrant of faith*. He maintained that the warrant to believe lies not in sinners themselves but in the invitations themselves. This surely is clear in such verses as: 'God now commands all people everywhere to repent' (Acts 17:30) and, 'And this is his command: to believe in the name of his Son, Jesus Christ' (1 John 3:23).

---

6   C. H. Spurgeon, *Metropolitan Tabernacle Pulpit*, 1861, vol. 7, 148. Spurgeon here claims all the Puritans to be on his side on the question of the free offer of the gospel.

7   C. H. Spurgeon, *The Early Years, 1834-1859* (Edinburgh: The Banner of Truth Trust, 1962), 364.

We note that Peter in his sermon at Pentecost exhorted *everyone* who was listening to repent and be baptized (Acts 2:38).

Hyper-Calvinists respond to this by arguing that if all are called to trust in Christ, then such trust must involve believing falsehood, because Christ did not die for all. Such preaching they claim denies particular redemption. (This issue is addressed in the following chapter.) Every sinner is responsible to repent and believe. In Luke 14:15-24 we read of the man who prepared a great banquet and invited many guests. He sent his servant to tell those who had been invited: 'Come; for everything is now ready.' But they all alike began to make excuses. And so with Christ, there is sufficiency in Christ's atonement to save all, but all do not want to come. The question of adequacy is never entertained in Scripture, simply because it is not a valid question. The apostles guarantee with one voice to all sinners everywhere that salvation is certain for those who repent and believe.

Third, Spurgeon affirmed the fact of human responsibility. This is the heart of the matter. The sinner's will has been crippled, but his responsibility has not been negated or annulled. Here is Spurgeon's eloquent summary of the matter:

> I do not think that I differ from any of my Hyper-Calvinistic brethren in what I do believe, but I differ from them in what they do not believe. I do not hold any less than they do, but I hold a little more, and, I think, a little more of the truth revealed in the Scriptures. Not only are there a few cardinal doctrines, by which we can steer our ship North, South, East or West, but as we study the Word, we shall begin to learn something about the North-west and North-east, and all else that lies between the four cardinal points. The system of truth revealed in the Scriptures is not simply one straight line, but two; and no man will ever get a

right view of the gospel until he knows how to look at the two lines at once. For instance, I read in one book of the Bible, 'The Spirit and the bride say, Come. And let him that heareth say, Come. And let him that is athirst come. And whosoever will, let him take the water of life freely.' Yet I am taught, in another part of the same inspired Word, that 'it is not of him that willeth, nor of him that runneth, but of God that sheweth mercy'. I see in one place, God in providence presiding over all, and yet I see, and I cannot help seeing, that man acts as he pleases, and that God has left his actions, in a great measure, to his own free-will. Now, if I were to declare that man was so free to act that there was no control of God over his actions, I should be driven very near to atheism; and if, on the other hand, I should declare that God so over-rules all things that man is not free enough to be responsible, I should be driven at once into Antinomianism or fatalism. That God predestines, and yet that man is responsible, are two facts that few can see clearly. They are believed to be inconsistent and contradictory, but they are not. The fault is in our weak judgement. Two truths cannot be contradictory to each other.[8]

---

8 Spurgeon, *The Early Years*, 176. I believe Spurgeon would whole-heartedly endorse J. I. Packer's book *Evangelism and the Sovereignty of God* (Downers Grove: InterVarsity Press, 1961).

10

SOVEREIGNTY, RESPONSIBILITY, AND EVANGELISM

Divine sovereignty and human responsibility have engaged the minds of theologians throughout the centuries. Perhaps the best way to grasp the combination of human responsibility in which everything seems to depend on us, and divine sovereignty in which everything depends on God, is to study texts such as Philippians 2:12-13: 'Continue to work out your salvation with fear and trembling (our responsibility), for it is God who works in you to will and to act according to his good purpose (divine sovereignty).'

Divine sovereignty precedes human responsibility. Every spiritual act we perform which is acceptable to God can be traced back to the divine initiative of grace. Both sovereignty and responsibility must be fully asserted. We must never make an excuse of God's sovereignty as the Jews did in captivity in Babylon. They did this in a subtle way, blaming their predecessors for the mess they were in and implying that God had been harsh. But they were really avoiding the fact that they themselves were to blame for their evil behaviour. Ezekiel drives home the fact that every individual is fully responsible for his own sin (Ezekiel 18). Indeed the Bible teaches everywhere that every person is responsible for his thoughts, words, and deeds — *everyone* will be held to account. Ecclesiastes concludes with this declaration: 'For God will bring every deed into judgement, including every hidden thing, whether it is good or evil' (Ecclesiastes 12:14). Revelation 20 describes the great judgement day and says that 'each person was judged according to what he had done' (Revelation 20:13; see also Matthew 21:31-36).

Largely fuelled by books published by the Banner of Truth publishing house (Edinburgh, Scotland), the doctrines of grace spread widely in the UK and America from about 1958 onwards. Suddenly, interest was quickened, and the issue of where divine sovereignty and human responsibility meet ascended to the top of the theological agenda.

The doctrines of grace have a profound impact on the way Christians evangelize and J. I. Packer addressed this subject at a series of meetings organized by a Christian Union in London in 1959. These papers were gathered together and appeared in print as a paperback with the title *Evangelism and the Sovereignty of God*.[1] Chapter two of this small book is titled, 'Divine Sovereignty and Human Responsibility'.[2] Packer suggests that we have to deal with an *antinomy*, which the *Shorter Oxford Dictionary* defines as 'a contradiction between conclusions which

---

1   J. I. Packer, *Evangelism and the Sovereignty of God* (Downers Grove, IL: Inter-Varsity Press, 1961).

2   Packer, *Evangelism and the Sovereignty of God*, 19.

seem equally logical, reasonable or necessary'. Packer writes,

> For our purposes, however, this definition is not quite accurate; the opening words should read 'an *appearance* of contradiction'. For the whole point of an antinomy — in theology, at any rate — is that it is not a real contradiction, though it looks like one. It is an *apparent* incompatibility between two apparent truths. An antinomy exists when a pair of principles stand side by side, seemingly irreconcilable, yet both undeniable. There are cogent reasons for believing each of them; each rests on clear and solid evidence; but it is a mystery to you how they can be squared with each other. You see that each must be true on its own, but you do not see how they can both be true together. Let me give an example. Modern physics faces an antinomy, in this sense, in its study of light. There is cogent evidence to show that light consists of waves, and equally cogent evidence to show that it consists of particles. It is not apparent how light can be both waves and particles, but the evidence is there, and so neither view can be ruled out in favour of the other.[3]

Many have found this way of explaining the compatibility of divine sovereignty and human responsibility very helpful. Throughout Scripture we see the absolute sovereignty of God. There are outstanding examples of this, such as the life of Joseph who was cruelly treated by his brothers and sold as a slave into Egypt. As we follow his life, step by step, it is enthralling to see that God is in control. From the depths of enslavement and prison, Joseph is eventually raised up and given the position of prime minister of Egypt.

---

3 Packer, *Evangelism and the Sovereignty of God*, 18-19.

The supreme example of divine providence is seen in the birth, life, death, and resurrection of our Lord Jesus Christ. In Acts we read that by the predetermined plan of God, he was nailed to a cross by the hands of godless men, and put to death (Acts 2:23).

As we follow the course of the life of Joseph and that of our Lord we observe that all those involved are accountable. Joseph's brothers were responsible for their actions. It was essential that they were brought to repentance. God used adversity to stir their consciences and bring them to confess their sins. Likewise in the life of our Lord, all those involved were accountable: Judas for betraying Jesus, Pilate for giving him up unjustly, and the Jewish leaders for their malevolence and wicked behaviour.

J. I. Packer's explanation of antinomy is very helpful, but perhaps the word 'tension' will serve as well.[4] In the case of antinomy there is the idea of mystery, of something we believe but cannot possibly resolve. With the word 'tension' is the idea that there is a problem, but with much thought, we might eventually understand how the issue of sovereignty and responsibility are compatible. My personal preference is antinomy.

The sovereignty of God should be employed as an *encouragement* to evangelism. We can see how this works out both personally and corporately as follows:

1. GOD'S SOVEREIGNTY SHOULD ENCOURAGE THE WORK OF PERSONAL EVANGELISM

It is easy to slip into this way of thinking, namely, God is sovereign and all-powerful and so he will save his elect people

---

4   This is the view of D. A. Carson who wrote a doctoral thesis 'Divine Sovereignty and Human Responsibility' at Cambridge University and then turned it into a more readable book called *Divine Sovereignty & Human Responsibility: Biblical Perspectives in Tension* (Marshall, Morgan and Scott, 1978).

without our assistance. This bypasses the fact that our sovereign, omnipotent God uses *means* to save his people. *He uses us!* The church is given the responsibility to evangelize at home and to promote missions abroad — that involves *all* of God's people. It is harmful to fall into the lazy mentality of ascribing the responsibility of evangelism and mission to just pastors and leaders. The reality is that *every Christian* will find themselves in environments where they are the only ones who know the gospel of salvation. It is incumbent on them to share the gospel with the unbelievers who surround them.

God gave this charge to Ezekiel, his prophet in Babylon:

> Son of man, I have made you a watchman for the house of Israel; so hear the word I speak and give them warning from me. When I say to a wicked man, 'You will surely die', and you do not warn him or speak out to dissuade him from his evil ways in order to save his life, that wicked man will die for his sin, and I will hold you accountable for his blood. But if you do warn the wicked man and he does not turn from his wickedness or from his evil ways, he will die for his sin; but you will have saved yourself (Ezekiel 3:17-19).

Every believer is responsible to bear witness to the saving gospel of Christ.

In his sovereignty, God has decreed that salvation comes by *hearing* the gospel. Paul writes:

> Everyone who calls on the name of the Lord will be saved. How, then, can they call on the one they have not believed in? And how can they hear without someone preaching to them? And how can they preach unless they are sent? As it is written, 'How beautiful are the feet of those who bring good news!' (Romans 10:13-15).

There are many living around us who will *never* hear the good news unless they hear it from us. In Western Europe only a tiny percentage attend church, and when they do attend they may only hear moralisms and not the saving gospel of Christ. Recently I listened to a BBC Radio Four's Lord's Day early morning Christian service from an Anglican church. The name of Christ was not even mentioned once throughout the service and even in the benediction they managed to avoid his name. Thankfully there are churches in the Anglican Communion where the gospel *is* faithfully preached. Sadly, in some denominations, the gospel has either been lost or is so obscure that no one is quite sure what it means.

In a secular society where evolutionary humanism and postmodernism prevail it is easy to become discouraged and be tempted to think that there is little we can do. It is now up to the sovereignty of God. No! The responsibility to be salt and light is always with God's people. Ezekiel in Babylon and Jeremiah in the environs of Jerusalem ministered in a time of declension. But these prophets did not falter in their active ministry, and they did not compromise the message that was given to them to preach.

2. GOD'S SOVEREIGNTY SHOULD ENCOURAGE ORGANIZED EVANGELISM BY THE CHURCH

This is an extension of the last point — from individual responsibility to the *corporate* responsibility of local churches. The Great Commission (Matthew 28:18-20) requires that the church use every means possible to advance the saving gospel of Christ. The avenues of evangelism vary from country to country. In some countries, particularly Islamic nations, propagating the Christian gospel is strictly forbidden. Under such circumstances it is easy to give way to the idea that God in his sovereignty has closed the doors and therefore we can do nothing. Radio ministry is one possibility. It is true that doors need to be opened but, in the meantime, we must never use the truth of God's sovereignty as an excuse for neglecting our responsibilities.

In countries where there is freedom to evangelize, it is often the case that churches do very little by way of organized, active evangelism — outreach to the community becomes neglected as does interest in and active support of overseas missions. The work of missions barely makes a spot on the agenda for the annual general meeting of some local churches. This neglect can be due to a wrong view of the sovereignty of God — the idea that he is all-powerful and will do his own work without our help. But he does not employ angels to carry the gospel message — he uses us! He does not normally use dreams to make the gospel known; it is very rare for souls to be awakened to their need by that means. I know of one case of a man finding an evangelical church by means of a dream. Would it not have been better if a Christian had taken the trouble to visit him?

The sovereignty of God is a powerful motive for evangelism. When Paul was facing stiff opposition at Corinth, the Lord spoke to him in a vision, 'Do not be afraid; keep on speaking, do not be silent. For I am with you, and no one is going to attack and harm you, because I have many people in this city' (Acts 18:9-10). God has many elect people. They must be found by reaching out to them in evangelism. Sowing is connected to reaping. As we read in Psalm 126, those who work hard will be rewarded: 'Those who sow in tears will reap with songs of joy. He who goes out weeping, carrying seed to sow, will return with songs of joy, carrying sheaves with him' (Psalm 126:5-6).

The sovereignty of God is a powerful motive in promoting missions abroad. It is through the sovereign power of God that the Holy Spirit was poured out on the day of Pentecost (Acts 2). There are features of Pentecost that make that event unique, but as an outpouring of the Holy Spirit, Pentecost was the first of many heaven-sent revivals that adorn the history of the church. In fact, every new surge forward of the gospel can be traced to an outpouring of the Holy Spirit. This is immensely motivational, because God is glorified in revivals by the gathering of multitudes of people to himself.

Motives for evangelism arise from compassion for the lost and from obedience to God's command in the Great Commission to 'go and make disciples of all nations' (Matthew 28:19). But supremely, the glory of God should motivate evangelism. There are many Scriptures that inspire prayer and effort. Psalm 86:9 declares: 'All the nations you have made will come and worship before you, O Lord; they will bring glory to your name.' A similar promise is found in Malachi 1:11: 'My name will be great among the nations, from the rising to the setting of the sun. In every place incense and pure offerings will be brought to my name, because my name will be great among the nations, says the LORD Almighty.' We should grip firmly these promises in prayer. Note Psalm 2:8, 'Ask of me, and I will make the nations your inheritance, the ends of the earth your possession', and Isaiah 62:6-7, 'You who call on the LORD, give yourselves no rest, and give him no rest till he establishes Jerusalem and makes her the praise of the earth.'[5]

3. GOD'S SOVEREIGNTY SHOULD NOT NEGATE THE FREE OFFER OF THE GOSPEL

This subject is mentioned in the chapter on Hyper-Calvinism, but here I ask the question, why do some show aversion to free offers of the gospel? The reason is that they have a misguided view of the sovereignty of God. They hold that it is

---

5 Expositions of how to plead the promises of a sovereign God are opened up in my book *Give Him No Rest: A Call to Prayer for Revival* (Darlington: Evangelical Press, 2006).

dishonouring to God to attribute what they call 'creature power' to the will of man because the sinner's will is a slave to sin and unbelief. They also think that it is dishonouring if God has to plead with the sinner who is depraved.

However, when we examine the passages of Scripture that describe the way in which lost humanity is addressed, there is nothing dishonouring to God in them. He reasons with sinners (Proverbs 1:22), invites them to come to him (Isaiah 55:1), offers wine and milk to them without price (Isaiah 55:1), and offers to make an everlasting covenant with those who repent and come to him (Isaiah 55:3). The word *offer* is used in the sense that if one party fulfils a condition the other party will keep his promise. Hence, when Peter exhorts the Jerusalem sinners to repent and be baptized, he promises that they will receive the gift of the person and work of the Holy Spirit. There is nothing amiss in construing that as an offer.

In addition, the Lord appeals to sinners and he implores them to repent (2 Corinthian 5:20). What is wrong with appealing and imploring? If you love people and you see them walking towards disaster, is it not appropriate to warn them and appeal and implore them not to go that way? If you have grown children and you see that they are courting disaster in their lives, do you not implore and appeal that they should desist from that behaviour? There is nothing dishonouring in doing that. Surely it would be dishonouring *not* to use every lawful means to persuade them away from taking a road that leads to disaster.

Some find great difficulty with Revelation 3:20: 'Here I am! I stand at the door and knock. If anyone hears my voice and opens the door, I will come in and eat with him, and he with me.' The Authorized Version reads: 'Behold, I stand at the door, and knock.' The word 'Behold' may sound old-fashioned but it is better than the exclamation mark in the NIV after the words 'Here I am!' It is remarkable that the Son of God should condescend to stand at the door and knock. That *is* something to behold! It is true that Arminian thinking can depict Christ as forlorn and helpless, standing in the cold and rain, dejected and rejected because the free will of the sinner refuses to let him in. There are some evangelists who are fond of using a famous Pre-Raphaelite painting by William Holman Hunt (1827-1910) as an illustration. It pictures Jesus standing outside a door with a lantern. He is knocking to gain entrance. But the handle of the door is on the *inside* of the door.

In order to escape the predicament of Christ having to stand at the door of the sinner's heart, some suggest that Revelation 3:20 is addressed to the church at Laodicea, not to individuals. Certainly the letter is addressed to that church, but the text addresses each individual directly as it says, 'If *anyone* hears my voice' (italics mine).

The correct way to interpret Revelation 3:20 is found in writers like the Puritan John Flavel (1628-1691) who loved this text so much that he preached a series of fourteen excellent sermons on it.[6] Flavel shows that hearing the voice of Christ at the door represents the effectual call. The text says, 'if anyone hears my voice'. That is an effectual call. The Bible describes Christ as quickening whomever he will (Matthew 11:27). There is nothing dishonouring for Christ to be patient or for his evangelists to be patient and persevering. Coming to Christ, opening the heart to Christ, is imperative in every conversion. The free invitations and exhortations in gospel preaching are God's way to achieve that.

In respect of gospel invitations, Charles Spurgeon is a model preacher. The love of God was in his gospel invitations. He was uninhibited, flexible, entreating and urgent in the way he addressed sinners. He commanded and he reasoned, he warned

6 John Flavel, *Works* (Edinburgh: The Banner of Truth Trust, 1982), 4:17-306.

and he pleaded in accord with the way the Scriptures address this issue.

Spurgeon's sermon, 'Compel them to come in', preached to a vast congregation in London at the Music Hall, Royal Surrey Gardens, on 5 December 1858 was wonderfully blessed by God. Spurgeon comments in the preface to volume five of the *New Park Street Pulpit*:

> The sermon entitled 'Compel them to come in' has been so signally owned of God, that scarcely a week occurs without some case of its usefulness coming to light. The violent, rigid school of Calvinists will, of course, abhor the sermon; but this is a very small matter when the Holy Ghost works by it in the salvation of men.

Here is an example from that sermon of how personal, urgent and direct Spurgeon was.

> My brother, I entreat you to stop and consider. Do you know what it is you are rejecting this morning? You are rejecting Christ, your only Saviour. 'Other foundation can no man lay'; 'There is none other name given among men whereby we must be saved'. My brother, I cannot bear that you should do this, for I remember what you are forgetting: the day is coming when you will want a Saviour. It is not long before weary months shall have ended, and your strength begins to decline; your pulse shall fail you, your strength shall depart, and you and the grim monster — death, must face each other. What will you do in the swellings of Jordan without a Saviour? Death-beds are stony things without the Lord Jesus Christ. It is an awful thing to die anyhow; he that has the best hope, and

the most triumphant faith, finds that death is not a thing to laugh at. It is a terrible thing to pass from the seen to the unseen, from the mortal to the immortal, from time to eternity, and you will find it hard to go through the iron gates of death without the sweet wings of angels to conduct you to the portals of the skies. It will be a hard thing to die without Christ. I cannot help thinking of you. I see you acting the suicide this morning, and I picture myself standing at your bed-side and hearing your cries, and knowing that you are dying without hope. I cannot bear that. I think I am standing by your coffin now, and looking into your clay-cold face, and saying, 'This man despised Christ and neglected the great salvation.'[7]

We can be sure that we will not be disposed to invite wayward transgressors to Christ, or reason with them, or address the over-tures of the gospel to them, unless we are convinced that God is favourably disposed to them and will have them to be saved.

The will of God that sinners should repent and turn to him is expressed in what we call the optative mood, that is the mood of desire or wish. God says, for example, 'If only you had paid attention to my commands, your peace would have been like a river, your righteousness like the waves of the sea' (Isaiah 48:18) and, 'Oh, that their hearts would be inclined to fear me and keep all my commands always, so that it might go well with them and their children for ever!' (Deuteronomy 5:29).

4. GOD'S LOVE FOR ALL IS AN ENCOURAGEMENT TO EVANGELISM

Hyper-Calvinists reject common grace and the idea that God loves all men and women. They believe that God loves the elect

---

7 C. H. Spurgeon, *New Park Street Pulpit* (1859), 5:21.

and hates the non-elect. We need to come to terms with the fact that the Scriptures declare the hatred of God for evil-doers. 'You hate all who do wrong', Psalm 5:5 says. This challenges us to look more carefully at the subject of God's love.

When John says, 'God is love' (1 John 4:8), that means that God is love in the three Persons of his being. The love and unity of the Trinity is a unity of perfect love. The Father loves the Son perfectly and completely, and the Son loves the Father similarly. The Holy Spirit loves perfectly and is united with the Father and the Son completely. This is the kind of unity into which we as believers are brought.

There are three ways in which we can understand the love of God at work. God loves complacently, benevolently, and graciously. The *benevolent* love of God is expressed in Psalm 145: 'The LORD is good to all; he has compassion on all he has made' (Psalm 145:9). This is sometimes referred to as the common grace of God. This is also clearly expressed in Acts 14:17: 'He has not left himself without testimony: he has shown kindness by giving you rain from heaven and crops in their seasons; he provides you with plenty of food and fills your hearts with joy.'

The *gracious* love of God is seen in his saving work. This stems from a love that achieves salvation against all opposition and obstacles. 'Many waters cannot quench love; rivers cannot wash it away' (Song of Solomon 8:7).

The *complacent* love of God means his love of delight. This love is vital in our understanding of the Trinity. The Father loves his Son supremely, perfectly, and unchangeably: 'You are my Son, whom I love; with you I am well pleased' (Luke 3:22). The Father loves the glories and merits of his Son. Christ, in turn, loves his Father perfectly. The three Persons of the Trinity are in love with each other. The Holy Spirit reveals the love of God (Romans 5:5) and searches the deep things of God (1 Corinthians 2:10). He loves the Father and the Son completely and eternally.

Into this circle of love, the church is brought — to be loved with a delight of pleasure. 'If anyone loves me, he will obey my teaching. My Father will love him, and we will come to him and make our home with him' (John 14:23). This love of delight is expressed through the prophet Zephaniah: 'The LORD your God is with you, he is mighty to save. He will take great delight in you, he will quiet you with his love, he will rejoice over you with singing' (Zephaniah 3:17). The church is in the process of being purified and being made beautiful as the bride of Christ and, as such, is the object of Christ's love (Revelation 21:2).

Love of delight in the attributes of God is the love of heaven. This is perfect love and will reign in the New Jerusalem and on the new earth.

In his book, *Love in Hard Places*,[8] D. A. Carson describes the various loves: the love of the Father for his Son, that is love within the Trinity; God's providential love over his entire universe; God's yearning, inviting, seeking love; God's electing love; and his conditional love, which has to do with our obedience. If we keep his commandments we will know in large measure God's love in adoption (John 14:21). We observe then that God's love is not all the same and neither is his hatred. Robert Sheehan reminds us that God never hates with a malevolent hatred, and he describes the difference between God's hatred of priority and God's judicial hatred. There are measures and degrees and variations during the course of time as God hates iniquity and treasures up his wrath against the day of wrath (Romans 2:5).[9]

God's benevolent love extends to all men and women, and

---

8 D. A. Carson, *Love in Hard Places* (Milton Keynes/Carlisle: Paternoster Press, 2002), 15ff. There is further helpful writing by Don Carson in 'How can we reconcile the love and the transcendent sovereignty of God?' in Douglas S. Hoffman and Eric L. Johnson, eds., *God Under Fire* (Grand Rapids: Zondervan, 2002).

9 Robert Sheehan, 'God's Love to the Non-Elect' in *Reformation Today*, 145:13.

the reason for this is explicitly declared in Romans: 'Or do you think lightly of the riches of his kindness and tolerance and patience, not knowing that the kindness of God leads you to repentance?' (Romans 2:4, NASB).

On earth, we humans alone are created in God's image. As a result we can understand the issues of love and hate described in this chapter. No chimpanzee or ape can read this chapter. I will conclude by illustrating the way in which love and hatred cross. There is a well-known Presbyterian theologian, Dr Nigel Lee, who was raised in South Africa but eventually settled in Australia. One day he received the appalling news that his ageing father, living on a farm in South Africa, had been murdered by a burglar. I have no doubt that hatred, not only for the crime itself, but for the murderer, rose in the heart of Nigel Lee. The police tracked down the murderer, and a judge sentenced him to many years in prison. Thereupon Nigel Lee took a flight from Australia to South Africa and obtained permission from the prison officers to evangelize the murderer. Nigel persevered with that murderer until he was soundly converted. Subsequent correspondence reveals that the murderer has not gone back on his profession of faith.

We also read of Jonah, who hated the Ninevites but was compelled to obey God and go and preach to them — and they repented. These examples show us that this matter of hatred and love is not easy to understand.

11

PERSEVERANCE AND APOSTASY

The Scriptures contain strong warnings against apostasy. There are five warning passages in Hebrews (2:1-4; 3:7-19; 5:11–6:12; 10:19-39; 12:14-29) that deliver both stern warnings and positive encouragement. The clearest and strongest of these passages are Hebrews 6:4-6 and 10:26-31. With regard to Arminianism, these passages have been the source of much difficulty, discussion, and controversy, probably more than any other parts of divine revelation. It is therefore important to open them up in detail.

Certainly Hebrews 6:4-6 and 10:26-31 seem to contradict the doctrine of the perseverance of the saints. These passages refer to those who have been greatly favoured and have had every appearance of being Christians but who, instead of improving their privileges, have abandoned the faith and brought shame and reproach to the name of Christ.

Hebrews 6:4-6 and 10:26-31 do not refer to shallow-ground hearers (Matthew 13:20-21) whose profession is superficial and they soon fall away. In some parts of the world easy believism is practised. This is when all that hearers of the gospel have to do is to put up their hands or walk down the aisle and make a decision for Christ. Thereupon they are declared to be Christians. Metaphorically speaking, that is like making hurdles six inches high for athletes who are expected to hurdle at the standard height of three foot six inches. That makes six-inch hurdles look ridiculous. Easy believism is sinister in its practice because it omits the necessity of heart repentance towards God, encourages shallow professions of faith, and promotes false assurance in those who are deceived by it.

In this chapter I first describe the nature of apostasy, secondly examine Hebrews 6:4-6 and 10:26-31, and thirdly reinforce the truth of perseverance.

WHAT IS APOSTASY?

Apostasy is when one who has every appearance of being a Christian goes back completely on his profession and practice of the faith. Judas Iscariot was an apostate. The opposite of perseverance is apostasy. The Greek word *apostasia* means a revolt, a standing away from, or a falling away. *Aphistemi* means to revolt, to depart, to fall away, and is used in various forms in the New Testament. The apostles warned against a coming general apostasy (2 Thessalonians 2:3; 1 Timothy 4:1-3; 2 Peter 3:17). The verb *parapipto* (fall away) is used in Hebrews 6:6. This word is used only once in the New Testament and means to fail to follow through with a commitment. It occurs in the Septuagint[1] in Ezekiel 14:13; 15:8; 18:24; 20:27. In these instances, a deliberate act of rebellion is conveyed by *parapipto*.

One of the most notorious apostates was Julian the Apostate (Flavius Claudius Julianus), Roman emperor from A.D. 361 to 363. Julian was educated in the Christian faith and practised Christianity. He built a chapel and conducted services (although there is no record of his baptism). Later, however, he reverted to paganism and became a bitter enemy of Christians and Christianity. When he became emperor, he excluded all Christians from public office, deprived the church of its privileges, and did all he could to restore pagan temples and pagan worship. That he was a sworn enemy of Christ is illustrated by the report that in the agonies of death, having been wounded in battle, he cried out, 'Thou hast conquered, O Galilean'. This points to the enmity to Christ that had been so strong in his later life.[2] Julian illustrates well what is involved in apostasy because he was one who knew much about the Christian religion but was never truly born again.

It is important to clearly distinguish between backsliding and apostasy. There is no word used in the Greek New Testament for backsliding, but it is often implied. There are four words in Hebrew for backsliding. Backsliding is implied in the Letter to the Hebrews. For instance, there are those who cease to attend regularly the stated meetings of the church (Hebrews 10:25). There are those who profess to be Christians but show little evidence of it in their lives. Backsliding is associated with weakness. Under pressure Peter denied Christ before a servant girl, but he repented deeply and was restored. The famous Archbishop Thomas Cranmer (1489-1556) under the threat of being burned at the stake weakened and denied his Protestant faith. He then repented and died with great

---

1 The Septuagint is the Greek version of the Old Testament.
2 For a biography of Julian the Apostate, see Schaff's *Religious Encyclopaedia*.

heroism in the flames. Likewise the Bohemian reformer and martyr, Jerome of Prague (1365-1416), under psychological torture at the Council of Constance denied his Protestant faith. However he recovered and when the flames crept up round him to consume his body at the stake Jerome sang the Easter hymn ('Hail, festal day') and repeated three articles of the Apostles' Creed concerning Father, Son, and Holy Spirit.

The reality of spurious faith or faith that falls short of union with Christ and regeneration is well attested in Scripture. For instance, John declares, 'They went out from us, but they did not really belong to us. For if they had belonged to us, they would have remained with us; but their going showed that none of them belonged to us' (1 John 2:19). This is surprising because it is suggested that not one or two but several left the faith. They did not transfer their membership from one church to another, which is a common occurrence today, but they left completely, perhaps to join a heterodox Gnostic cult. This reference to a number leaving raises a vital issue, which is the difference between personal apostasy, individual by individual, which is the subject of this chapter, and corporate apostasy. There have been periods in church history when doctrinal standards have been eroded and Christian holiness compromised so badly that the gospel has been lost. This was the case prior to the sixteenth-century Reformation. All the Reformers and all the English Puritans held the position that 2 Thessalonians 2 foretells the apostasy from apostolic Christianity as seen in the rise and dominance and corruption of the papacy. Whether we hold to that interpretation of 2 Thessalonians 2 or not, no one can deny that a major corporate apostasy from apostolic Christianity took place over the centuries prior to the Reformation.[3] In more recent times, liberal theology represents

---

3 The Reformed view of the papacy as antichrist is expounded and defended in 'The Puritans and the Promises' by Erroll Hulse, Westminster Conference Papers, 1999.

a major apostasy from biblical Christianity.[4] But now we return to the subject of personal apostasy.

The vivid parable of the sower and the seed (Matthew 13:18-23) tells of four types of soil representing four different responses to the gospel. One kind of seed falls by the wayside and the birds of the air eat it up. These are those who hear the Word, but the devil soon removes the impression made. The seed that falls on rocky places is the man who hears the Word and at once receives it with joy; but, since he has no root, he lasts only a short time. When trouble or persecution comes because of the Word, he quickly falls away. The one who received the seed that fell among thorns is the man who hears the Word, but the worries of this life and the deceitfulness of wealth choke it, making it unfruitful. But the one who received the seed that fell on good soil is the man who hears the Word and understands it. He produces a crop, yielding a hundred, sixty or thirty times what was sown.

This parable symbolizes different kinds of hearers. Because it is a parable of metaphors, it is misguided to suggest, that since the seed that fell into shallow ground or among thorns actually took root, it represents the new birth.

The parable fits well with the observations of pastors. In my experience I have noted the accuracy of this parable in describing different responses to the Word. It is the seed that fell among thorns which comes closest to apostasy. This represents the man who hears the Word, but the worries of this life and the deceitfulness of wealth choke it, making it unfruitful. Does this hearer represent the apostate? Those represented here seem to fall short of attaining full commitment with

---

4 In John J. Murray, *Catch the Vision: The Roots of the Reformed Recovery* (Darlington: Evangelical Press, 2007), Murray analyzes the decline in historic Christianity during the first half of the twentieth century. The spread of liberalism and Arminianism resulted in the evangelical church losing her vision of God in his glory and sovereign grace that characterized her witness in former times.

the church and union with Christ and with God's people.

If we allow for those who fall into sin but then repent, as has been discussed above, then it must be noted there are very few outright apostates, that is, hardly any who fit the description of Hebrews 6:4-6 and 10:29-31. The reason why I use the word 'outright' is because the term apostasy is often used to describe those who fall into sin. But a fall into sin may not lead to outright apostasy. Many pastors have fallen morally. Most of them have come to repentance, some sooner, and others after several years. For believers who have been right in the heart of church life to become apostate is truly rare. C. H. Spurgeon, in 'Sermon 75' in his New Park Street sermons, uses the word 'if' from the KJV to suggest that this kind of apostasy does not really happen. It is only hypothetical. The 'if' is not in the Greek text. Donald Guthrie in his commentary published by InterVarsity Press takes the participle 'falling away' in a hypothetical sense as though apostasy is hypothetical and does not really happen. Hence Guthrie takes Hebrews 6:4-6 as a solemn warning even though apostasy does not occur. However apostasy *is* a reality. It is rare. There was only one Judas. But apostasy is a reality.

This subject shows how important it is to process carefully everyone who applies for believers' baptism and church membership. What are the ingredients of a credible profession of faith? The main issues concern genuine repentance towards God and faith in the Lord Jesus Christ. With regard to faith in Christ, discernment is needed as to whether faith is mere knowledge about Christ or is it the faith of a living union with Christ? Are there ulterior motives? It has been known for individuals to make a profession of faith in order to gain a wife or a husband. Then there is the case of those who flee persecution from Islamic countries in whom there is often a great desire to gain refugee status. Membership with a Christian church is perceived as an advantage for gaining that status.

Evangelical churches usually show love and care. Evangelical Christianity is attractive compared with the harshness and legalism of Islam. But evangelical Christianity as a mere religion must be carefully distinguished from what it is for an individual believer to experience and sustain a living, day-by-day union with Christ.

HEBREWS 6:4-6 EXAMINED

This Scripture reads:

> It is impossible for those who have once been enlightened, who have tasted the heavenly gift, who have shared in the Holy Spirit, who have tasted the goodness of the word of God and the powers of the coming age, if they fall away, to be brought back to repentance, because to their loss they are crucifying the Son of God all over again and subjecting him to public disgrace (Hebrews 6:4-6).

The first expression used is: 'have once been enlightened'. There are those who hear and understand the truth of the gospel but this understanding falls short of salvation. Their understanding of the gospel is with the mind and not with the heart. It is purely intellectual. The writer is warning his readers against the very real danger of *knowing* the truth but not *obeying* it from the heart.

The second expression used is: 'who have tasted the heavenly gift'. What is the heavenly gift? The texts, 'God so loved the world that he gave his one and only Son' (John 3:16), and 'He who did not spare his own Son, but gave him up for us all' (Romans 8:32) affirm the truth that Christ is God's gift from heaven. But there are several passages that declare that the Holy Spirit is the gift from the Father and the Son to the church. On the day of Pentecost, Peter said, 'Repent and be baptized, every one of you, in the name of Jesus Christ for the forgiveness of your sins. And you will receive the gift of the Holy Spirit' (Acts 2:38). The same Peter rebuked Simon Magus for thinking he could buy the gift of the Holy Spirit with money (Acts 8:20).

What then is meant by 'heavenly' in the phrase 'heavenly gift'? In 1 Peter 1:12 we read of 'the Holy Spirit sent from heaven'. I am constrained to take 'who have tasted the heavenly gift' to refer to the Holy Spirit but agree that this seems strange when the next phrase is 'who have shared in the Holy Spirit'. It need not, however, be regarded as repetitious when we remember that often in Scripture one phrase is followed by another to reinforce a truth. 'Sharing in the heavenly gift' points to the fact that a person can realistically share in the Holy Spirit and yet be unregenerate and unsaved. This was the case with Balaam who delivered remarkable prophecies: 'When Balaam looked out and saw Israel encamped tribe by tribe, the Spirit of God came upon him and he uttered his oracle' (Numbers 24:2). Likewise, the Holy Spirit came upon King Saul and he prophesied (1 Samuel 10:10). It is clear from his later life that King Saul was apostate. He became completely consumed with jealousy of David, which led to the most appalling murder of the innocent priests of Nob (1 Samuel 22:6-23). At the time of his death, instead of seeking the Lord Saul consulted a witch.

Hebrews 6:4-6 forms a solemn warning that *gifts* of the Holy Spirit are not the same as the *fruit* of the Spirit. In recent times there have been major scandals when famous television evangelists who boasted of great gifts fell into sin and have been exposed as adulterers and money-lovers. Jesus warns,

> Not everyone who says to me, 'Lord, Lord', will enter the kingdom of heaven, but only he who does the will of my Father who is in heaven. Many will say to me

on that day, 'Lord, Lord, did we not prophesy in your name, and in your name drive out demons and perform many miracles?' Then I will tell them plainly, 'I never knew you. Away from me, you evildoers!' (Matthew 7:21-23).

A Christian should be recognized by his godly life and not by charismatic gifts. The apostle John, in his first letter, insists on *three essential marks of a true Christian*. He must believe that Christ is divine, he must live a holy life, and he must love the brethren. False Christians often pass the first test but fail morally and often fail to integrate with the Christian family and show true love for the body of Christ, the church.

Finally there are the words, 'who have tasted the goodness of the word of God and the powers of the coming age'. As already explained, this is not referring to shallow-ground hearers who soon fall away. These are those who enter fully into the life of the church. There may well be a reference here to the miraculous gifts and displays of power witnessed in primitive Christianity. Those who love sensational healing meetings are susceptible to living by external excitements rather than the stringent disciplines of the heart required by the Word of God. Those who major in sensations are susceptible to falling away from the church altogether when scandals or divisions occur. They become bitter and can become hostile to the gospel, which is the essence of apostasy. They evidence the reality that they were never born again.

HEBREWS 10:26-31 EXAMINED
This warning reads:

If we deliberately keep on sinning after we have received the knowledge of the truth, no sacrifice for sins is left, but only a fearful expectation of judgement and of raging fire that will consume the enemies of God. Anyone who rejected the law of Moses died without mercy on the testimony of two or three witnesses. How much more severely do you think a man deserves to be punished who has trampled the Son of God under foot, who has treated as an unholy thing the blood of the covenant that sanctified him, and who has insulted the Spirit of grace? For we know him who said, 'It is mine to avenge; I will repay', and again, 'The Lord will judge his people' (Hebrews 10:26-31).

This solemn warning against apostasy in Hebrews stresses the truly terrible judgement that comes on one who enjoyed the central privileges of Christ but who then trample them underfoot to shame Christ and shame his church.

The perplexing phrase is: 'who has treated as an unholy thing the blood of the covenant that sanctified him'. How can one who has been sanctified apostatize? 'Sanctify' is used in different ways in the New Testament. As far as the local church is concerned, when a believer is baptized that signifies the separation of that believer into Christ. The first and basic meaning of 'to sanctify' is 'to set apart'. It also means 'to make holy on the inside'. The first meaning here is to be taken, namely, 'to be set apart'. It does not mean an internal regeneration. This person was set apart. For all intents and purposes, we all regarded the baptism of this person as proceeding on a sincere basis and a credible profession of faith. This person was accepted into church membership and participated in the activities of the church, such as the Lord's Supper. Then followed the falling away, either gradually or suddenly.

In turning away from Christ the apostate tramples the Son of God under foot, and treats as an unholy thing the blood of the covenant that sanctified him. It is regularly affirmed at the communion service that the wine represents the shed blood of Christ. 'This is my blood of the new covenant which is shed for many' (Matthew 26:28, NKJV). In the communion, the wine is called 'the blood of the new covenant'. 'This cup is the new covenant in my blood' (1 Corinthians 11:25). According to Hebrews 9:23-28, the blood of Christ is the foundation or basis of all the Father's gracious provisions of salvation for his people. Therefore, rejecting the blood of the covenant, for one who has understood its meaning and publicly professed personal reliance on it for salvation, is apostasy. In the words of John Owen this is 'the absolute height of all sin and impiety that the nature of man is capable of'.[5] The judgement meted out to the apostate will be severe and in proportion to that wickedness.

A REINFORCEMENT OF THE TRUTH OF PERSEVERANCE

Arminianism maintains that a person can be truly born again and then for various reasons fall away and then be damned for ever. On the face of it, Hebrews 6:4-6 and 10:26-31 seem to support that. But as we have seen, when the passages are examined more closely, they describe those who lack the regenerating work of the Holy Spirit. The Arminian view is widely held. It is the doctrinal position of Methodists, Roman Catholics, the Salvation Army, Holiness churches, and some Pentecostal churches. The Apostolic Church makes acceptance of this doctrine a condition of church membership. John Wesley even goes so far as to say: 'to retain the grace of God is much more than to gain it. Hardly one in three does this'.[6] This is the view of R. C. H. Lenski, the well known Lutheran Bible commentator. On John 10:27-29, Lenski states: 'we ourselves may turn wilfully from him and may perish wilfully of our own accord'.[7]

---

5 John Owen, *Hebrews* (Edinburgh: The Banner of Trust Trust, 1991).

6 John Wesley, *Journal*, July 1774.

7 R. C. H. Lenski, *The Interpretation of St. John's Gospel* (Grand Rapids: Hendrickson, 1998), 756.

It is terrifying for a Christian to think that he might apostatize and be eternally lost. What if he comes into unendurable tribulation and his will breaks? What if he is tortured and is overcome? What if illness attacks him and he loses his sanity and his grip? The Bible addresses these fears and does so on the basis of God's grip on us. Paul writes to the Philippians and assures them: 'being confident of this, that he who began a good work in you will carry it on to completion until the day of Christ Jesus' (Philippians 1:6).

This good work of God, begun and carried on to completion, is sustained by perseverance. Perseverance is expressed consistently in the New Testament. The key word used for perseverance in the New Testament is *hypomonê*, meaning patience, endurance, perseverance (*meno* 'I remain', *hypo* 'under'), hence remaining steadfast under pressure. *Hypomonê* is sometimes translated by the word 'endurance'.

It will help to observe some notable instances of its occurrence in the New Testament. One key instance is our Lord's affirmation, 'Because of the increase of wickedness, the love of most will grow cold, but he who stands firm (*hypomeinas*, endures) to the end will be saved' (Matthew 24:12-13). Perseverance is an integral part of the believer's spiritual equipment and character. It is the basic attitude of the righteous. Perseverance is also mentioned in the parable of the sower: 'But the seed on good soil stands for those with a noble and good heart, who hear the word, retain it, and by persevering produce a crop' (Luke 8:15, see also Romans 2:7).

Perseverance as part of the Christian life is affirmed by Paul in Romans 5:3: 'suffering produces perseverance; perseverance, character'. Likewise James reminds us, 'the testing of your faith develops perseverance' (James 1:3) and, 'Blessed is the man who perseveres under trial, because when he has stood the test, he will receive the crown of life that God has promised to those who love him' (James 1:12). Again James says, 'we consider blessed those who have persevered', and he uses Job as a model of one who persevered in an exemplary manner (James 5:11).

Peter, in outlining a way of certainty against falling away, requires of us that we 'make every effort to add to your faith goodness; and to goodness, knowledge; and to knowledge, self-control; and to self-control, perseverance; and to perseverance, godliness; and to godliness, brotherly kindness; and to brotherly kindness, love' (2 Peter 1:5-7). Peter goes on to say that if we build these disciplines into our lives we 'will never fall, and will receive a rich welcome into the eternal kingdom of our Lord and Saviour Jesus Christ' (2 Peter 1:10-11).

However the Letter to the Hebrews is the principal source of teaching on the theme of perseverance in the Bible. From first to last its style is one of admonition to persevere and avoid apostasy. Psalm 95:7-11 is cited in Hebrews 3:7-11 and 4:3-11. The writer reminds the Hebrews that they did stand their ground (10:32) — they persevered (*hypemeinate*). They are exhorted to persevere in the race (12:1), remembering that Christ endured appalling agony for us (12:3). They should know and appreciate that the endurance (*hypomenete*) of chastening as sons, is an essential part of the Christian life (Hebrews 12:7-11).

We see throughout the New Testament that perseverance and endurance (*hypomonê*) are an essential part of our Christian experience.[8] Jesus said, 'My sheep listen to my voice; I know them, and they follow me. I give them eternal life, and they shall never perish; no one can snatch them out of my hand.

---

8 '*Hypomonê* as the basic attitude of the righteous, as developed in the Old Testament and later Judaism finds a natural continuation in the eschatologically oriented thinking of the New Testament. The endurance which is given with hope of the realization of the kingdom of God is a basic attitude of the Christian as he faces attacks of a hostile and unbelieving world and as he finds himself in the midst of its temptations. It is a decisive precondition to attain personally to the final salvation of God' (Kittel, vol. 4, 581).

My Father, who has given them to me, is greater than all; no one can snatch them out of my Father's hand. I and the Father are one' (John 10:27-30). Further, we have the promise: 'Never will I leave you; never will I forsake you' (Hebrews 13:5).

The well-known hymn, 'How firm a foundation, ye saints of the Lord', expresses beautifully the promises that we find in Isaiah 43:2-3 and Hebrews 13:5:

> When through the deep waters I call thee to go,
> The rivers of woe shall not thee overflow;
> For I will be with thee, thy troubles to bless,
> And sanctify to thee, thy deepest distress.
>
> When through fiery trials thy pathway shall lie,
> My grace, all-sufficient, shall be thy supply;
> The flame shall not hurt thee; I only design
> Thy dross to consume, and thy gold to refine.
>
> The soul that on Jesus has leaned for repose
> *I will not, I will not* desert to its foes;
> That soul, though all hell should endeavour to shake,
> *I'll never, no never, no never forsake!* [9]

To this assurance must be added the certainty of the new covenant which is set before us in Hebrews 8:8-12. The difference between this new covenant and the old covenant made with the house of Israel is this: they broke that covenant, whereas we will never break the new covenant, because God's laws are written on our hearts and on our minds. As we see from the vivid descriptions in Jeremiah and Ezekiel, the nation of Judah apostatized. The great majority of people turned away from the Lord to serve idols. I will never

---

9 Stanzas from 'How firm a foundation, ye saints of the Lord' by 'K—' in John Rippon, ed., *A Selection of Hymns by the Best Authors*, 1787.

fall away because God's law is written on my mind and in my heart.

The safety of a small child crossing a ravine with his father is not the child's grip on his father's hand but rather the strong hand of his father's grip on him. That illustrates our position as God's children. We hold as tight as we can, but in our weakness we depend on the faithfulness of our Father and the certainty of his love and purpose. This reality is echoed in these verses by Augustus Toplady:

> The work which his goodness began,
>   The arm of his strength will complete;
> His promise is 'Yea' and 'Amen'
>   And never was forfeited yet:
> Things future, nor things that are now,
>   Nor all things below or above,
> Can make him his purpose forgo,
>   Or sever my soul from his love.
>
> My name from the palms of his hands
>   Eternity will not erase;
> Impressed on his heart it remains
>   In marks of indelible grace:
> Yes, I to the end shall endure,
>   As sure as the earnest is given;
> More happy, but not more secure,
>   The glorified spirits in heaven.[10]

---

10 Stanzas from 'A debtor to mercy alone' by Augustus Toplady.

12

GOD WANTS YOU TO BE SAVED

Salvation, as we saw in the first chapter, is justification by faith, holiness of life, and assurance of a glorious resurrection to eternal life. The way to this salvation is by repentance from sin and faith in our Lord Jesus Christ. *Do you have this salvation?*

If you do not have salvation then I assure you that God wants you to be saved. Perhaps you are a reader who lacks assurance of salvation. Or perhaps you are a reader who thinks along the lines that there is little hope since the majority are lost and few are saved. But I assure you that God wants you to be saved. Does God desire the salvation of all the lost, that is, every one of them? 1 Timothy 2:4 declares that God our Saviour 'wants all men to be saved and to come to a knowledge of the truth'.

The Father wants you to be saved. Christ Jesus would have you be saved. The Holy Spirit strives for you to be saved. We will consider God the Father first.

THE FATHER WANTS YOU TO BE SAVED

God commanded Ezekiel to proclaim to the people: 'As surely as I live, declares the Sovereign LORD, I take no pleasure in the death of the wicked, but rather that they turn from their ways and live. Turn! Turn from your evil ways! Why will you die, O house of Israel?' (Ezekiel 33:11). The background to this statement is that the people were blaming their forefathers for their exile in Babylon. And they were accusing God of injustice:

> Yet you say, 'The way of the Lord is not just'. Hear, O house of Israel: Is my way unjust? Is it not your ways that are unjust? If a righteous man turns from his righteousness and commits sin, he will die for it; because of the sin he has committed he will die. But if a wicked man turns away from the wickedness he has committed and does what is just and right, he will save his life (Ezekiel 18:25-27).

The Lord repudiates the accusation that he is unjust. He makes it crystal clear that each person is responsible for his own sin. It is futile to engage in blame-shifting. The exhortation follows: 'Rid yourselves of all the offences you have committed, and get a new heart and a new spirit. Why will you die, O house of Israel? For I take no pleasure in the death of anyone, declares the Sovereign LORD. Repent and live!' (Ezekiel 18:31-32).

From this we can establish the following principles:[1]

---

1 Richard Baxter, *A Call to the Unconverted*. This book has been transposed into contemporary English and republished by Evangelical Press with the title *An Invitation to Live* (1991). The principles have been extracted from the latter.

1. It is an unchangeable law of God that the wicked must turn from their wickedness or they will be condemned.
2. God promises that if the wicked will turn, they will receive eternal life.
3. God takes pleasure in a person's conversion and salvation, not in their death or damnation; he had rather they would turn to him and live than persist in their sin and die.
4. God is so concerned that men should not question these truths that he solemnly confirms with an oath that he has no pleasure in the death of the wicked.
5. God is so concerned for the conversion of sinners that he repeats his commands to turn and live.

'He is patient with you, not wanting anyone to perish, but everyone to come to repentance', writes Peter (2 Peter 3:9). If, after all this, sinners refuse to turn, it is not God's fault that they perish. The reason they perish is their own sinfulness. They are damned because they choose to be.

God says, 'Rid yourselves of all the offences you have committed, and get a new heart and a new spirit. For why will you die, O house of Israel? For I take no pleasure in the death of anyone, declares the Sovereign LORD. Repent and live!'

This surely is impossible! How can I give myself a new heart? The command is 'repent and live'! If you repent, you will live. The text is designed to bring you to an end of yourself so that you look to the cross of Christ for cleansing and salvation. You must repent or be damned. You can't repent because you are gripped by sin. There is only one way out of this tension ('I must but I cannot') and that is to look up to God for his deliverance.

CHRIST JESUS WOULD HAVE YOU BE SAVED

Christ's love and compassion was revealed in his unremitting labours, healing and teaching, preaching and organizing preaching tours (Luke 10:1ff). His ministry is summed up in Romans 10:21: 'But concerning Israel he says, "All day long have I held out my hands to a disobedient and obstinate people." ' A division of that text suggests itself as follows:

1. How did Christ preach? *He stretched forth his hands in invitation.*
2. When did Christ so preach? *All the day long.*
3. To whom did Christ so preach? *To a disobedient and obstinate people.*

Even after Jesus had done many miracles in the presence of the Jews they still would not believe in him. He reasoned with them and said, 'I have come into the world as a light, so that no one who believes in me should stay in darkness' (John 12:46). He went on to say, 'I did not come to judge the world, but to save the world' (John 12:47, NASB). In his commentary on the Gospel of John, John Calvin writes,

> Why then did Christ not wish to condemn them? Because he had temporarily laid aside the office of judge and offers salvation to all indiscriminately and stretches out his arms to embrace all, that all may be encouraged to repent. And yet he heightens by an important detail the crime of rejecting an invitation so kind and generous; for it is as if he had said: 'See, I have come to call all; and forgetting the role of judge, my one aim is to attract and rescue from destruction those who already seem doubly ruined.'[2]

What was Christ's declared purpose? The answer: 'to save the world'. This is confirmed by the statement: 'For God did

---

2   John Calvin, (trans. T. H. L. Parker) *The Gospel According to St John 11 – 21 and The First Epistle of John* (Edinburgh: Oliver and Boyd, 1961), 52.

not send his Son into the world to condemn the world, but that the world through him might be saved' (John 3:17, NKJV). On the words, 'that whosoever believes on him should not perish', Calvin says,

> The outstanding thing about faith is that it delivers us from eternal destruction. For he especially wanted to say that although we seem to have been born for death sure deliverance is offered to us by the faith of Christ so that we must not fear the death which otherwise threatens us. And he has used a general term, both to invite indiscriminately all to share in life and to cut off every excuse from unbelievers. Such is also the significance of the term 'world' which he had used before. For although there is nothing in the world deserving of God's favour, he nevertheless shows he is favourable to the whole world when he calls all without exception to the faith of Christ, which is indeed an entry into life.[3]

How can you know that Jesus would have you to be saved? The answer is clearly seen in the way he viewed his opponents in Jerusalem. His enemies behaved in a hateful, vindictive way, yet Jesus desired them to be saved. We remember that as Jesus approached Jerusalem and saw the city, he wept over it and said,

> If you, even you, had only known on this day what would bring you peace — but now it is hidden from your eyes. The days will come upon you when your enemies will build an embankment against you and encircle you and hem you in on every side. They will

---

3   John Calvin, (trans. T. H. L. Parker) *The Gospel According to St John 1 – 10* (Edinburgh: Oliver and Boyd, 1959), 74

dash you to the ground, you and the children within your walls. They will not leave one stone on another, because you did not recognise the time of God's coming to you (Luke 19:41-44).

Jesus' tears over these people prove his desire that you should be saved. What a terrible thing it is to go into a lost eternity bearing the guilt of your sins! How awful to be lost for ever and for ever knowing that salvation was in reach and that Christ would have you saved. How desperately sad to be found among those to whom he stretched out his hands in invitation to come to him and find rest, but like those unbelieving Jews over whom Jesus wept, you too will be lost.

Jesus did not come to judge. He will not condemn now. He has postponed the judgement and given time for repentance.

John Calvin interprets Christ's meaning in John 12:48 as follows: 'Because I burn with a great desire for your salvation, I refrain from my right of condemning you.'[4] Who would not interpret Christ's tears over reprobate Jerusalem as desire for anything other than their salvation? Does he not lament the fact that they had missed the great day of their visitation? The day of opportunity was over. Salvation was now hidden from their eyes. The judicial blindness from God was upon them. Their stubbornness had led to God himself hardening their hearts and blinding their eyes (John 12:40). Jesus said of his own people, the Jews, 'How often I have longed to gather your children together, as a hen gathers her chicks under her wings, but you were not willing' (Matthew 23:37).

If Jesus grieved over the unrepentant sinners of Jerusalem you can be sure he grieves over you if you are unbelieving and unrepentant. His desire is that you will be saved.

Our time on earth is a day of probation and hence of

---

4 Calvin, *The Gospel According to St John 11 – 21*, 53.

opportunity. The time allotted to men and women is called 'the last days'. Until the coming judgement of Jesus Christ this is a time of proclamation of the gospel to every creature. This is the time of the salvation of the world. The time is coming when Christ will judge the world. Until then it is a time of universal proclamation of the gospel and universal preaching, a time, in fact, of heightened responsibility for all hearers. And so great is the personal responsibility involved in rejecting what constitutes wholehearted invitations and offers of mercy, that the judgement will be very severe and terrible for those who reject them, just as it was for the Christ-rejecters of Jerusalem. If these invitations were insincere they would be hypocritical and sinful, but God cannot sin. He cannot be accused of duplicity. The judgement was worse for the Christ-rejecters of Jerusalem because they received the offers of mercy from the very lips of the God-man himself. The gospel heightens human responsibility immensely. Christ will return with flaming fire on those who do not obey the gospel (2 Thessalonians 1:8, NKJV).

The cynic can say that if Christ came to save the whole world he must be frustrated, because it is obvious he has failed in that objective. It is true that, on the face of it, our Lord's ministry seemed to have little fruit by way of numbers. It is fatal to think in terms of majorities. Time and time again in history the majority opinion has proved to be wrong. The majority put their trust in a pacifist approach to Nazi Germany before the Second World War and were proved to be wrong.

The rejection of Jesus by the Jews was overruled for good inasmuch as the gospel then spread to the Gentile nations. It is unwise to talk in terms of defeat until we see the final outcome, which is yet to be. The full extent of salvation in the earth has yet to be seen. Note these words from the prophet Isaiah:

And now the LORD says, — he who formed me in the womb to be his servant to bring Jacob back to him and gather Israel to himself, for I am honoured in the eyes of the LORD and my God has been my strength — he says: 'It is too small a thing for you to be my servant to restore the tribes of Jacob and bring back those of Israel I have kept. I will also make you a light for the Gentiles, that you may bring my salvation to the ends of the earth' (Isaiah 49:5-6; see also Romans 11; Psalm 72; Habakkuk 2:14).

While North America and Western Europe are in a state of spiritual and moral decline, a vast spiritual harvest is being gathered in Africa, Asia, Latin America, and especially China, which is experiencing the most extensive spiritual revival in the history of the Christian church. When Jesus said he came to save the world he meant it!

The eternal world will be inhabited by a number so great it will be difficult to count. There will be numbers there from every tribe, language, nation, and people group on this planet. There is room for you. It is clear that Jesus is 'the way and the truth and the life' (John 14:6). Since he has made the once-and-for-all propitiation for sin he is the *only* way to the Father: 'Salvation is found in no one else, for there is no other name under heaven given to men by which we must be saved' (Acts 4:12). The way of repentance and faith is urged for you too.

THE HOLY SPIRIT STRIVES FOR YOU TO BE SAVED

In Genesis 6:5 we read, 'The LORD saw how great man's wickedness on the earth had become, and that every inclination of the thoughts of his heart was only evil all the time.' In the same context we read, 'Then the LORD said, "My Spirit will not contend with man forever, for he is mortal"' (Genesis 6:3). This text can be understood as an assertion that the Holy Spirit strives with sinners and that there is a limit as to how long he will strive. There are difficulties in interpreting the Hebrew text, but it is a fact that the Holy Spirit does strive with sinners.[5] The reason why he strives with them is that he will have them to be saved.

When Stephen, the first Christian martyr, preached to the unbelieving Jews, he told them that they were stiff-necked and had uncircumcised hearts and ears. Stephen said to them, 'You are just like your fathers: You always resist the Holy Spirit! Was there ever a prophet your fathers did not persecute?' (Acts 7:51-52).

What was the work of the Holy Spirit that they resisted? It was a striving with them to repent of sin and accept the saving truth that God would give them salvation in the person of the coming Messiah. Jesus said, 'Every sin and blasphemy will be forgiven men, but the blasphemy against the Spirit will not be forgiven' (Matthew 12:31). This terrible sin that will not be forgiven is the act of rejection of perfectly clear evidence. The Pharisees committed this unpardonable sin. They witnessed firsthand the miracles of Jesus but then attributed those miracles to Satan (Matthew 12:22-32). We must not grieve the Holy Spirit when he comes to persuade us to believe and live.

The Spirit's work is to convince us of sin, of righteousness and of judgement to come. These are the great issues. It is hard work to convince a sinner that he is guilty and needs to repent. Even those in prison for proven crimes are often self-righteous and maintain that they are at least better than others and point to those who have committed worse crimes. The Ten Commandments prove to our consciences that we are guilty before God. Note what Paul says in Romans:

---

5 John D. Currid in his commentary on Genesis [*Genesis: Volume 1* (Darlington: Evangelical Press, 2003)] takes the text to mean 'my Spirit will not remain' referring to the fact that God is promising to withdraw life from mankind. Matthew Henry and many other commentators accept the translation as it is.

> Let no debt remain outstanding, except the continu-
> ing debt to love one another, for he who loves his fel-
> low-man has fulfilled the law. The commandments,
> 'Do not commit adultery', 'Do not murder', 'Do not
> steal', 'Do not covet', and whatever other command-
> ment there may be, are summed up in this one rule:
> 'Love your neighbour as yourself'. Love does no harm
> to its neighbour. Therefore love is the fulfilment of
> the law' (Romans 13:8-10).

Apply this to yourself. Jesus said that to lust in our hearts is
the same as committing adultery (Matthew 5:27-28). He also
showed that to hate others in our hearts carries the seeds of
murder and is the same kind of sin as murder (Matthew 5:21-
22). Do you break these commandments? Go through the Ten
Commandments one by one and you will soon see how you
transgress them.

We also break God's law by falling short in the rule of love:
'"Love your neighbour as yourself." Love does no harm to its
neighbour. Therefore love is the fulfilment of the law' (Romans
13:9-10). We fall far short of what we should be in our love
for others. We fall short in loving even those closest to us.
How often in your life has a bad mood caused you to be hurt-
ful to those whom you should love?

The Holy Spirit convinces us of our sins and of our sinful
lives. He convinces us of our need to believe in Christ for
salvation. By nature we resist conviction of sin and resist
coming to faith in Christ. We are afraid because allegiance to
him will be costly. Yet the Holy Spirit persists in his work to
convince us that we must believe.

The Holy Spirit especially convicts us of unbelief. Rejection
of the truth is the greatest sin of which a man is capable. Unbelief is a sin that, if persisted in, will end in eternal damnation
(John 3:36). It is the sin against the one and only remedy there

is for us to be saved. Unbelief is the basic sin. Unbelief puts self at the centre of things and consequently refuses to believe.[6] This is the world's most characteristic sin. The sin of unbelief and its consequences is seen in that God sent his Son into the world to his own people and his own people did not receive him. Men love darkness rather than light. Man's will is enslaved to his passions. That enslavement is the root cause of unbelief.

Sin is a sensitive issue. We are shamed by it. We resent having to face the reality of our sins. There are many painful issues we would prefer to face before facing up to our sinful guilt before God. Because it is his desire to save us, the Holy Spirit perseveres in his work to bring us to confess our sins and forsake them.

Our sinful state and the guilt of our sins means that we are destitute of righteousness before God. The Holy Spirit convinces us of our need of righteousness and reveals that this need is provided perfectly in the imputed righteousness of Christ. The Holy Spirit reveals the only righteousness that can save (Romans 1:17). He reveals this because he wants us to be saved.

The Holy Spirit further convicts us of our need to be saved because of the coming universal judgement: 'When the Son of Man comes in his glory, and all the angels with him, he will sit on his throne in heavenly glory. All the nations will be gathered before him, and he will separate the people one from another as a shepherd separates the sheep from the goats. He will put the sheep on his right and the goats on his left' (Matthew 25:31-33). The outcome of this great judgement day is awesome. 'Then he will say to those on his left, "Depart from me, you who are cursed, into the eternal fire prepared for the devil and his angels"' (Matthew 25:41).

---

6 Leon Morris, *The Gospel According to John* (Grand Rapids: Eerdmans, 1995), 698.

Why continue under the dominion of sin and Satan? The Holy Spirit assures us that a decisive victory has been won over Satan: 'Now the Prince of this world will be driven out' (John 12:31)[7] and 'The reason the Son of God appeared was to destroy the devil's work' (1 John 3:8). Victory over sin and Satan is ours when we become Christ's disciples. The Spirit wants you to become a disciple. He wants you to believe in Jesus and be saved.

---

7 Herman Ridderbos is helpful in his emphasis that John 16:8-11 needs to be read within the context of the then prevailing contest between Christ and Satan. Satan is about to be dealt a decisive defeat: 'Now the Prince of this world will be driven out' (John 12:31). Our Lord was preparing his disciples for his departure against the background of a hostile world which does not believe in him. This rejection extended to the violence of the crucifixion. In this, the Christ-rejectors side with Satan. But Satan is defeated at the cross [Herman Ridderbos, *The Gospel of John: A theological commentary* (Grand Rapids: Eerdmans, 1991)].

WHAT THE BIBLE TEACHES ABOUT BEING BORN AGAIN

BY GARY BRADY

In many parts of the world today you will meet people who say they are 'born again Christians'. Numerous individuals claim to be 'reborn' or 'regenerate'. Every so often, the media report that some celebrity or other has been 'born again'. Pollsters suggest that as many as 80-90 million Americans claim to be born again. This book is written with the intention of helping those who want to study the subject from a biblical point of view. If, as we believe, the new birth is entering 'a new world, a new state of existence', with 'a new capacity for action' — then it is something we all need to know about and something we all need to understand clearly, whether we have experienced it or not.

ISBN 978-0852346747 • 175 PGS

www.epbooks.org

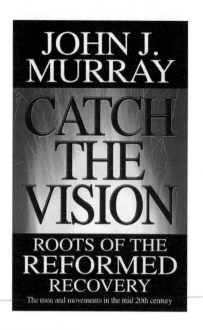

CATCH THE VISION
The roots of the Reformed recovery

BY JOHN J. MURRAY

A significant change came about in the history of the church in the United Kingdom in the middle decades of the twentieth century. It was by and large a recovery of something that had been a reality in the church in past generations. Step by step, men were led to see what was missing in the type of Christianity that prevailed for the first half of the century and began to direct their minds back to the glories of past eras. This book traces these providential links in the men and in the books that set in motion a recovery of the vision — looking at figures such as W. J. Grier, A. W. Pink and E. J. Poole-Connor. The central place is given to the influences that shaped the message and ministry of the leading figure in the recovery, Dr Martyn Lloyd-Jones.

ISBN 978-0852346679 • 191 PGS

www.epbooks.org

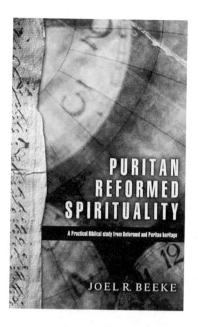

PURITAN REFORMED SPIRITUALITY

A practical theological study from our Reformed and Puritan heritage

BY JOEL R. BEEKE

Dr Beeke provides us with a first-class tour of some of the great sites of Reformed theology and spirituality. Here we meet John Calvin, Dr William Ames, Anthony Burgess and such Scotsmen as John Brown of Haddington, Thomas Boston and the remarkable brothers, Ebenezer and Ralph Erskine. Our guide then brings us to The Netherlands and to the time of the *Nadere Reformatie*, before taking us to the New World in the company of Theodorus Freylinghuysen. But the climax of this tour brings us to the family roots from which all these theologians and pastors came — to the strong foundations of Christian living in justification by faith and sanctification in life, nourished by the power of biblical preaching.

ISBN 978-0852346297 • 475 PGS

www.epbooks.org

Buying EP Books
supports
EP Mission,
Thank you.
www.epbooks.org

A wide range of excellent books on spiritual subjects is available from EP Books. Please write to us for your free catalogue or contact us by email.

EP PUBLISHING WITH A MISSION

EP Books
Faverdale North, Darlington, DL3 0PH England
EP Books USA
P. O. Box 825, Webster, NY 14580 USA
email: sales@evangelicalpress.org

www.epbooks.org